a different image

*To Lynn
from Betty and Al*

a different image

the legacy of broadside press • an anthology

Gloria House, Rosemary Weatherston, and Albert M. Ward

udmp
university of detroit mercy press

bp
Broadside Press

Detroit, USA • MMIV

Designed by Timothy Dugdale/Atomic Quill (www.atomicquill.com) in The Dudley Randall Center for Print Culture

NATIONAL ENDOWMENT FOR THE ARTS

udmp
university of detroit mercy press

bp
Broadside Press

michigan council for arts and cultural affairs

Library of Congress Cataloguing-in-Publication Data
A different image : the legacy of Broadside Press : an anthology /
[edited by] Gloria House, Rosemary Weatherston, and Albert M. Ward.-- 1st ed.
    p. cm.
Includes bibliographical references.
ISBN 0-911550-97-6 (trade pbk.)
1. American poetry--African American authors. 2. American poetry--20th century. 3. African Americans--Poetry. 4. Broadside Press. I. House, Gloria, 1941- II. Weatherston, Rosemary, 1967- III. Ward, Albert Michael. IV. Broadside Press. V. Title.

PS591.N4D54 2004
811'.5080896073--dc22
                          2004016118

For Gwendolyn Brooks, Etheridge Knight, Audre Lorde, and Dudley Randall.

Contents

introduction • gloria house   13

gwendolyn brooks   21

Introduction • Gloria House   22
kitchenette building   27
when you have forgotten Sunday: the love story   28
love note I: surely   29
the progress   30
The Bean Eaters   31
We Real Cool   32
The Lovers of the Poor   32
The Ballad of Rudolph Reed   37
Malcolm X   40
Fire, from The Third Sermon on the Warpland   41
An Aspect of Love, Alive in the Ice and Fire   42
The Life of Lincoln West   43
To Don at Salaam   49
Paul Robeson   50
The Boy Died in My Alley   51
Elegy In a Rainbow   53
A Black Wedding Song   54
Horses Graze   55
"When Handed a Lemon, Make Lemonade"   57
Friend   58

etheridge knight   61

Introduction • Albert M. Ward   62
Hard Rock Returns to Prison from the Hospital for
   the Criminal Insane   67
He Sees through Stone   68
The Idea of Ancestry   70
Haiku   72
To Make a Poem in Prison   74
As You Leave Me   75
Portrait of Malcolm X   76
To Dinah Washington   77
For Langston Hughes   78
To Gwendolyn Brooks   78
Apology for Apostasy?   79
Genesis   79
Another Poem for Me   80
Relaxing in the Charity Ward at Mercy Hospital   82
A Poem to Be Recited   83
No Moon Floods the Memory of That Night   84
Belly Song   85
This Poem   89
For Black Poets Who Think of Suicide   91
Jazz Drummer   91
A Poem for Myself   92
The Bones of My Father   93
Cop-out Session   95

audre lorde 97

Introduction • Willie Williams 98
For Each of You 107
Equinox 109
Black Mother Woman 112
The Seventh Sense 113
Teacher 114
Moving Out or The End of Cooperative Living 117
Generation II 120
Conclusion 121
The Winds of Orisha 122
Who Said It Was Simple 125
To My Daughter The Junkie On A Train 126
Now 128
Love Poem 129
Separation 130
Even 130
Revolution Is One Form Of Social Change 131
All Hallows Eve 132
Viet-Nam Addenda 133
Sacrifice 134
Blackstudies 136

haki madhubuti 145

Introduction • Sondai K. Lester 146
THE NEW INTEGRATIONIST 151
"STEREO" 152
RE-ACT FOR ACTION 153
FIRST IMPRESSIONS ON A POET'S DEATH 154
Gwendolyn Brooks 156
But He Was Cool or: he even stopped for green lights 158
DON'T CRY, SCREAM 160
Malcolm Spoke/ who listened? 166
a poem to complement other poems 167
blackmusic/a beginning 170
A Message All Blackpeople Can Dig 172
We Walk the Way of the New World 174
Move Un-noticed to be Noticed: A Nationhood Poem 178
Re-taking the Takeable 182
LIFE-STUDIES 183
WORLDVIEW 183

dudley randall 187

Introduction • Hilda Vest 188
Ballad of Birmingham 193
Memorial Wreath 195
Old Witherington 196
George 197
A Different Image 198

Dressed All In Pink   199
Roses and Revolutions   200
The brightness moved us softly   201
My second birth   202
The profile on the pillow   202
Anniversary Words   203
On Getting a Natural   204
Pacific Epitaphs   205
Poet   210
African Suite   211
To The Mercy Killers   214
Frederick Douglass and the Slave Breaker   214
Courage: A Revolutionary Poem   215
For Gwendolyn Brooks, Teacher   216
Green Apples   216
I Loved You Once   217
Tell It Like It Is   218
Blood Precious Blood   218
Litany of Friends   219
Poor Dumb Butch   223
The Ones I Love   224
Loss   224
To Be in Love   225
Women   226
The New Woman   226
In Africa   228
Bag Woman   228
A Poet Is Not a Jukebox   230
When I Think of Russia   233

sonia sanchez   237

Introduction • Jessica Care Moore   238
malcolm   244
to all sisters   246
personal letter no. 2   247
liberation/poem   248
Blk/Rhetoric   249
Indianapolis/Summer/1969/Poem   251
It's a New Day   253
to P. J. (2 yrs old who sed write a poem for me
     in Portland, Oregon)   254
we can BE   255
and it will be ours   256
woman   257
earth mother   259
young/black/girl   260
young womanhood   264
womanhood   273
We are Muslim Women   275

epilogue • rosemary weatherston   280

acknowledgements   284

Introduction

The age
requires this task:
create
a different image;
re-animate
the mask.

Shatter the icons of slavery and fear.
Replace
the leer
of the minstrel's burnt-cork face
with a proud, serene
and classic bronze of Benin.

(Dudley Randall "A Different Image")

In *Broadside Memories: Poets I Have Known* (1975), Broadside Press founder Dudley Randall wrote the following concerning his vision and mission as a writer and publisher: "We [Africans in the United States] are a nation of twenty-two million souls, larger than Athens in the Age of Pericles or England in the age of Elizabeth. There is no reason why we should not create and support a literature which will be to our own nation what those literatures were to theirs" (32). Though Randall never imposed his politics on the poets he edited and published, this statement and the consistency of his editorial practice over the years reveal his nationalist passion to cultivate the work of African American creative writers, to bring their poems into the homes of African American people by making the publications affordable, and, further, to extend this literature to the hearts of people around the world.

Dudley Randall created Broadside Press "by trial and error," he said, as a solitary project at first, perhaps not realizing how demanding the work would become, all the while continuing to work full-time in his profession of reference librarian. During those early days, the late Pulitzer prize-winning poet, Gwendolyn Brooks, a close friend of Randall's, wanted to know his title within the Broadside Press organizational structure. He replied: "[S]ince I in my spare time and in my spare bedroom, do all the work, from sweeping floors, washing windows, licking stamps and envelopes, and packing books, to reading manuscripts, writing ads, and planning and designing books . . . just say that Dudley Randall equals Broadside Press" (28). However, Randall did have the support of friends and other cultural activists who were employed as his assistants during various periods, including the young poets Melba Boyd and Jill Witherspoon Boyer, and office managers Bill Whitsitt and Malaika Wangara.

Operating in this modest manner, Randall began by producing 8 ½ x 11 inch broadsides on which single poems were printed in attractive formats, an idea he borrowed from the Russians, whose tradition of making popular poems and songs available to the people at minimal cost he had learned of during a trip to the Soviet Union. The first broadsides sold for under a dollar and subsequent books were priced as reasonably. For example, Audre Lorde's collection, *From a Land Where Other People Live*, published by Broadside in 1973 and nominated for a National Book Award in 1974, sold for only $1.50.

"Ballad of Birmingham," Randall's poem on the bombing deaths of four little girls in a Birmingham church during the civil rights movement, was the first Broadside, published in 1965. In the decade following, Broadside Press grew into one of the world's finest literary collections, with over one hundred titles, most of which were poetry. However, Randall had also developed the excellent Broadside Critics Series of literary criticism by outstanding scholars such as Addison Gayle and Houston Baker, as well as the Broadside Voices Series, which featured recorded performances by Haki Madhubuti, Sonia Sanchez, and others, precursors to the contemporary performance poetry movement.

The Broadside Collection included some surprises: a cookbook, *A Safari of African Cooking* (1972); a play for television by Detroit writer, Regina O'Neal (1974); and several children's books. Significant prose works in the inventory included Haki Madhubuti's first book of political analysis and commentary, *From Plan to Planet: Life Studies: The Need for Afrikan*

Minds and Institutions (1973), and Ms. Brooks's *Report from Part One* (1971), the first part of her autobiography. Randall also distributed works of thirty African diasporan poets of the Paul Breman Heritage Poetry Series, published in England.

By the mid-seventies, the Broadside repertory—more than a hundred single broadsides, as well as books, audio tapes, LP's, and posters—were in demand by individuals, bookstores, libraries, and universities around the world. For example, over eighty thousand poetry books of Don L. Lee (now Haki Madhubuti) were in circulation during this period, and Randall struggled to keep up with demands for new editions.

The work involved in building the Press had been a monumental effort, which, one might have foreseen, finally exhausted Randall as it enriched all of us. He needed to rest. Through the interventions of Haki Madhubuti, whose own Third World Press was thriving by then, Broadside Press came under the guardianship of a religious and cultural organization in Detroit, the Alexander Crummell Center for Worship and Learning. I coordinated a collective of volunteers at the Crummell Center, and we relocated the inventory to the Church basement, began to fill the mail orders, and, with the cash flow, paid off the debt to Harlo Printing, a local company where most Broadside books had been produced. The Crummell Center collective also ensured ongoing visibility for the Press by organizing regular cultural programs for the community, including writing workshops, readings by poets of national prominence such as Nikki Giovanni, and a Broadside Lecture Series that welcomed scholars such as Harold Cruse, author of *Crisis of the Negro Intellectual* (1967), Dr. Safisha Madhubuti, and many others. In keeping the Press alive in this manner, we showed Dudley Randall that the community treasured his work and awaited his return to health, factors that we believe contributed positively to his recovery.

After a few years, Randall was ready to resume an active role. He published *Songs for Maya* (1982) by Melba Boyd, and my first book of poems, *Blood River* (1983). He also instituted the Broadside Poets' Theatre, which still runs every third Sunday of the month under the direction of Willie Williams, a Broadside Press board member.

In 1985, Hilda and Don Vest purchased the Press from Dudley Randall. Hilda Vest, a poet who was a friend of Randall's and involved in the Broadside Press activities at the Crummell Center, and her husband Don, an experienced businessman and cultural activist, moved the Press office to Lafayette Street in downtown Detroit. They continued the Broadside Poets' Theater, won state funding to institute the successful Poet-in-Residence Program in collaboration with the Detroit Public Libraries, and secured additional grants to fund poetry projects for various underserved populations in the city. The Vests published fourteen new titles: two first books by young poets, Ray Waller (*Abstract Blues*, 1988) and Leslie Reese (*Upside Down Tapestry Mosaic History*, 1987); *Sorrow's End* (1993), poems by Mrs. Vest; *Wine Sip and Other Delicious Poems* (1989), by Sharon Knight-Smith; *Watermelon Rinds and Cherry Pits* (1989), by Murray Jackson; *Patches on Mainstreet* (1989), by Albert Ward; a children's coloring book on Grenada, *Island Images* (1989), and a poetry collection, *Riffin' to a Maroon Tune* (1996), both by Michelle Gibbs; *Hipology* (1990), an anthology of poems by Detroit metropolitan area writers, edited by Stella Crews and Ron Allen; two plays by Bill Harris, *Riffs & Coda* (1990); *Reflections: An Oral History of Detroit* (1992), by Irene Rosemond; poems by well-known Detroit medical doctor, William Chavis, *Designs/Lines* (1995); a collection of poems by Paris-based poet, James Emmanuel, *Jazz: from the Haiku King* (1999); and my second poetry collection, *Rainrituals* (1989). Under the Vests' direction, Broadside Press reclaimed its key role as publisher of excellent writings by African Americans, while continuing its legacy as a cultural haven for writers excluded from mainstream publishing opportunities. The Vests sold the Press to a collective of cultural activists in 1998: Richard Donelan, Ed.D.; Sondai Lester; Lindiwe Lester; Aombaye Ramsey, Ph.D.; Tene Ramsey; and Willie Williams and myself, both of whom had been Broadside Board members during the Vests' direction of the Press, and volunteers during the Crummell Center guardianship years.

As a whole, the Broadside Collection represents three generations of poets: Randall, Gwendolyn Brooks, Margaret Walker, Margaret Danner, Robert Hayden, Sterling Brown, and their peers in the Black literary community, whose works laid the foundation; the younger poets of the Black Consciousness era, including Sonia Sanchez, Willie Kgositsile, Nikki Giovanni, Alice Walker, Haki Madhubuti, Etheridge Knight, and Audre Lorde, who all later won national and international acclaim; and a still younger generation whose works emerged in the eighties. The poetry of these three generations comprises a repository that reflects the important political and cultural issues of African American society from the first world war to the end of the century, expressed in diverse literary forms—including revolutionary manifestos, exquisite love songs, humorous toasts, and yearnings for freedom. The entire enterprise is a testament to Randall's editorial acumen and respect for artistic differences within the African American community.

Beginning with Randall's investment of genius and hard work, continuing through the years at the Alexander Crummell Center, the tenure of Hilda and Don Vest, and the subsequent assumption of ownership by the collective identified above, Broadside Press has promoted the works of African American writers in the United States and throughout the world over a period of forty years. This anthology is meant to cast new light on this exceedingly valuable literary tradition, and to acquaint contemporary poets with the literary gold mine of their Broadside predecessors.

In founding the Press as an independent cultural institution with the writing and publication of "Ballad of Birmingham," a protest against the inhumanity of Southern racism, Randall conjoined Broadside Press and the African American freedom fight during a period when liberation struggles were being waged throughout Africa, Asia, and in Latin America. Colonized people worldwide, some engaged in armed struggle against European powers, were consolidating their national cultural and political movements, and working to build international solidarity as the Third World—rejecting alignment with both the Western camp and the Soviets, perceived as the first and second "worlds." The African American civil rights and Black power movements of the sixties and seventies constituted a significant flank of this global uprising of oppressed peoples, with many viewing these movements as a national liberation struggle, as they began to think of African Americans as an internal colony of the United States.

The tenacity of racial prejudice, the relentlessness of organized violence against Blacks throughout American society, and the intransigent segregation prevalent in all major arenas of American life—the courts, housing, education, employment—had convinced many in the generation that came to young adulthood in the sixties that African Americans would never win equal treatment as citizens of the United States. Alienated by the closed door of American whiteness and racial oppression, persistent for four centuries, African American political activists, intellectuals, and writers of the period sought their true identity elsewhere. They turned to Africa, the Motherland. With unprecedented intensity, Black artists and writers in all parts of the Diaspora attempted to wrest themselves psychologically from the hold of Eurocentric conventions, to forge a new aesthetic based on African arts cultural practices and spiritual traditions. This shift of focus resurrected latent nationalist sentiment of Blacks in the United States and generated the powerful Black Consciousness and Black Arts movements of the sixties and seventies.

Identification with Africa reconfigured all aspects of daily life for the "conscious" of this generation—including acceptance of one's own African physical features; reclamation of African clothing, art and artifacts, music, dance, and religion; commitment to the freedom struggle within the United States; and solidarity with the national liberation fighters on the African continent. There were other important concerns as well: African American women, who played major roles in the Black Consciousness movement, were redefining gender relationships and the goals of women's liberation— towards greater equality and respect between themselves and their men and towards a clear articulation of the ways in which their own political aspirations differed from those of Euro-American feminists. Protest against the war in Vietnam, which ranged from street demonstrations to draft resistance, expressed the consistent solidarity of African American artists and activists with Third World independence struggles. All these political developments may be traced in the recurring themes of the Broadside poetry featured in this anthology.

Fundamental to the Black Consciousness movement was the project of retrieving precolonial African history in order to reassert the role of African civilization onto the world stage, for therein lay fulfillment of the quest for personal and collective African American identity. Emerging African and African American scholars brought to light the magnitude of African history buried by Western cultural supremacist scholarship. They exposed the unprecedented horrors of the European trade in human beings and pointed out the direct relationship between this human exploitation and the accumulation of capital that would ensure European and American powers their subsequent imperialist stature in the world. This intellectual work laid the ideological basis for African American political resistance that took many forms. It also planted the seeds of the student demands of the seventies and eighties to bring Black Studies into the academy.

This anthology features six Broadside Press writers of the Black Consciousness era whose works we here refer to as classics: Gwendolyn Brooks, Etheridge Knight, Audre Lorde, Haki Madhubuti, Dudley Randall, and Sonia Sanchez, all of whom are recognized as major twentieth-century poets. Though they came to prominence in the 1960s and 1970s, the issues that preoccupied them are still pertinent to our communities today, and their writings continue to enjoy worldwide demand. They articulated the deepest longings of their people—to express their African identity and to assume their place in history. Moreover, they demonstrated a quality of craftsmanship that would set new literary standards. While improvising on traditional literary forms, they also initiated unique uses of English to render it truer to African American speech patterns and rhythms, an intimation of the affirmation that Black English would garner years later.

A new generation of poetry writers and lovers have now created the phenomenal "slam" poetry competitions and hundreds of new poetry performance venues throughout this country. At Broadside, we celebrate the emergence of these young writers, cultivating and supporting their work in our monthly Broadside Poets' Theatre and Workshop. We hope this Broadside Legacy anthology will be for them and others a source of inspiration for continued creativity and literary production.

Gloria House, Ph.D., Detroit
June 1, 2004

Works Cited

Randall, Dudley. *Broadside Memories: Poets I Have Known*. Detroit: Broadside Press, 1975.

gwendolyn brooks

Gwendolyn Brooks: Poet and Nationbuilder
Gloria House

Gwendolyn Brooks loved simple things and things of exquisite beauty. This is evident in the elegance of her poetic craft. She fashioned poems as a jeweler might work the facets of a gem: polishing the edges for brilliance and clarity of reflection; chiseling the language to its essence, as in the poem "Malcolm X"; jolting the imagination with improbable metaphors—as in "The Lovers of the Poor," where an apartment building is: "Oh Squalor! This sick four-story hulk, this fibre / With fissures everywhere! . . ." (75-6).

Ms. Brooks's early poetry featured city life and tenements, her own urban tribe of black folk, "oaken . . ., mustard colored . . ., low-brown butterballs," and dignified "bean-eaters," whom she brought to the center stage of American literature. Her rendering of her people's life into works of art was magnificent, and won her the Pulitzer Prize in 1950. Over fifty subsequent years of life, she remained her modest self, while the world acclaimed and honored her: as Poet Laureate of Illinois, as recipient of seventy-five honorary doctorates, as Consultant to the Library of Congress, as Fellow of the American Academy of Poets. These tributes did not loosen her tenacious roots in the Black community, or blind her to the understanding she expressed in her poem for Raul Robeson:

> we are each other's
> business:
> we are each other's
> magnitude and bond. (14-17)

Gwendolyn Brooks's legacy challenges writers to recognize the bond of community, history, and mission, to place their work firmly within the necessary struggles of their people, as she began to do during the Black Consciousness era.

In Ms. Brooks's embrace of young writers and activists of the period, her strong solo voice found its chorus. I imagined their camaraderie in the following way, and wrote the following lines to celebrate it:

Brave solo virtuoso
encounters youthful chorus,
embraces call and response,
steps to the *griot* center,
grows deeper, magnificent.

("Gwendolyn Brooks")

One shouldn't conclude that Ms. Brooks became politically conscious *only after* her engagement with the Black Consciousness movement, as some critics suggest, for a tightly reined-in fury over injustice and the arrogance of the rich had always run like steel through her poetry, as in "The Lovers of the Poor," where the pretensions of wealthy white women who feign charity are exposed as hypocrisy. The new element in her poetry during the seventies was that it began to reflect the presence of a *community* of artists and intellectuals who were together evolving an ideology of Black political commitment, and that this community was also the audience to which her focus seemed to shift entirely. Her poetry began to celebrate leading figures in that community—"Malcolm X" (dedicated to Dudley Randall), "Paul Robeson," "To Don at Salaam" (for poet Don L. Lee [Haki Madhubuti]), "To Keorapetse Kgositsile" (a South African poet in exile in the United States)—while espousing the principles of self-determination for an oppressed people. In "Elegy In a Rainbow," she expressed her longing for the full realization of this community as the African American Nation, whose existence she already recognized, though many of her generation remained faithful to the idea of integration.

By 1980, with the publication of *Primer for Blacks*, Ms. Brooks had assumed the *griot* center among her kinfolk, with preachments calling us to glory in our Blackness. In the title poem she wrote:

Blackness
is a title,
is a preoccupation,
is a commitment Blacks
are to comprehend—

and in which you are
to perceive your Glory. (1-7)

Black consciousness required a reevaluation of everything, for Western cultural hegemony had imposed values and aesthetics according to which Africans were viewed as inferior. Ms. Brooks's poetry undertook the ideological struggle necessary for restoration of African self-respect on all levels, including the very personal. In "For Those of My Sisters Who Kept Their Naturals" (also in *Primer for Blacks*), she praises Black women who do not straighten their hair, or otherwise yield to the pressure to look white, prizing European beauty over their own natural attributes. This was a central theme of the Black Consciousness movement:

> Sisters!
> I love you.
> Because you love you.
> . . . .
> You never worshiped Marilyn Monroe.
> You say: Farrah's hair is hers.
> You have not wanted to be white. (1-3, 23-25)

In addition to the ideological teachings, Ms. Brooks gave her audience humor, wisdom, and love, as seen in poems like "A Black Wedding Song," which blesses young couples and offers guidance in sustaining a marriage; "The Boy Died in My Alley," a lament for all the Black boys who are shot down anonymously in an oppressive system; "Horses Graze," which teases us gently for lacking insights that even animals appear to possess; and '"When Handed a Lemon, Make Lemonade,"' a playful instruction on enduring life's trials. As we read Ms. Brooks's work, we find that most of the important issues in modern life are touched upon—from loving to lynching, raising babies to abortion, from examples of human resourcefulness to images of self-destruction, as in her famous poem "We Real Cool." She treats all these subjects with deep understanding and technical mastery.

I remember my first readings of Ms. Brooks's poetry. Five or six of us students at the University of California, Berkeley used to get together on Saturday evenings to teach ourselves our African American heritage, for these were days before we could study our culture in American universities. We read Ms. Brooks's poems, and when the University invited her for a major literary presentation, we were overjoyed. We ventured up to her after her reading, invited her to tea, and spent a long evening talking literature in my bare apartment on Ashby Street.

The gift Ms. Brooks gave us young aspiring writers that night—her presence, interest, and belief in us—was a way of life for her. In the call and response of our encounter, elder to youth, master artist to apprentices, she affirmed that we were, indeed, heirs to a vibrant legacy, that fulfillment of our potential as artists was required and necessary to our *community*, not only to our individual aspirations. I have come to understand that the experience of our little group in Berkeley was only one example of Ms. Brooks's consistent lifetime practice of mentoring young writers.

From the Black Consciousness period until her passing, Ms. Brooks's attention remained focused on the project of African cultural restoration and nation building. She chose to publish her poetry through independent Black companies like Broadside Press and Third World Press, rather than mainstream houses. She awarded prizes to encourage young writers from her own personal income. She supported independent African American institutions, including those that would sustain ongoing literary study and production, such as the Gwendolyn Brooks Center for Black Literature and Creative Writing at Chicago State University. She was generous in her recognition of contemporary Black artists through awards and other tributes.

In December 2000, Ms. Brooks died of cancer at the age of eighty-three. Hundreds gathered at the auspicious Rockefeller Chapel of the University of Chicago on December 11th for her wake and funeral services. We listened to the taped music of Sweet Honey in the Rock's "Breaths." The lyrics of this song, translated from the French of the poem "Souffles," by Senegalese poet Birago Diop, express the African belief in the continuity and availability of the spirit after death:

Listen more often to things than to beings . . .
Those who have died have never left . . .
The dead are not under the earth
They are in the rustling tree . . .
They are in the baby's cry. . . . (1, 8, 11-12, 30)

As Sweet Honey's music faded, the drums of the Muntu Dance Company could be heard in the apse, and the dancers, dressed in ritual white, began a magnanimous performance of the West African Lamba, processing down the long aisle toward the altar. Artists young and old, community leaders and state dignitaries, family members and friends rose to the podium to speak their love for this lover of our people. Then, in full realization that a great soul had passed into the world of Spirit, we filed out of the Chapel into the surprising beauty of a snow storm, which had laid a thick cover, shutting down Chicago's afternoon traffic, creating an appropriately ominous silence.

Works Cited

Brooks, Gwendolyn. *Primer for Blacks*. Chicago: Brooks Press, 1980.

Diop, Birago. *"Souffles." Luerres et Lueurs, poemes commences en 1925*. Paris: *Presence Africaine*, 1960. 64-6.

Kgositsile, Aneb (Gloria House). "Gwendolyn Brooks." *Shrines*. Chicago: Third World Press, 2004. 31.

Sweet Honey in the Rock. "Breaths." Rec. 1981. *Breaths*. Flying Fish Records, 1992.

kitchenette building

WE ARE things of dry hours and the involuntary plan,
Grayed in, and gray. "Dream" makes a giddy sound, not strong
Like "rent," "feeding a wife," "satisfying a man."

But could a dream send up through onion fumes
Its white and violet, fight with fried potatoes
And yesterday's garbage ripening in the hall,
Flutter, or sing an aria down these rooms

Even if we were willing to let it in,
Had time to warm it, keep it very clean,
Anticipate a message, let it begin?

We wonder. But not well! not for a minute!
Since Number Five is out of the bathroom now,
We think of lukewarm water, hope to get in it.

when you have forgotten Sunday: the love story

——And when you have forgotten the bright bedclothes
   on a Wednesday and a Saturday,
And most especially when you have forgotten Sunday—
When you have forgotten Sunday halves in bed,
Or me sitting on the front-room radiator in the limping afternoon
Looking off down the long street
To nowhere,
Hugged by my plain old wrapper of no-expectation
And nothing-I-have-to-do and I'm-happy-why?
And if-Monday-never-had-to-come—
When you have forgotten that, I say,
And how you swore, if somebody beeped the bell,
And how my heart played hopscotch if the telephone rang;
And how we finally went in to Sunday dinner,
That is to say, went across the front room floor to the
   ink-spotted table in the southwest corner
To Sunday dinner, which was always chicken and noodles
Or chicken and rice
And salad and rye bread and tea
And chocolate chip cookies—
I say, when you have forgotten that,
When you have forgotten my little presentiment
That the war would be over before they got to you;
And how we finally undressed and whipped out the light
   and flowed into bed,

And lay loose-limbed for a moment in the week-end
Bright bedclothes,
Then gently folded into each other—
When you have, I say, forgotten all that,
Then you may tell,
Then I may believe
You have forgotten me well.

love note
I: surely

SURELY you stay my certain own, you stay
My you. All honest, lofty as a cloud.
Surely I could come now and find you high,
As mine as you ever were; should not be awed.
Surely your word would pop as insolent
As always: "Why, of course I love you, dear."
Your gaze, surely, ungauzed as I could want.
Your touches, that never were careful, what they were.
Surely—But I am very off from that.
From surely. From indeed. From the decent arrow
That was my clean naïveté and my faith.
This morning men deliver wounds and death.
They will deliver death and wounds tomorrow.
And I doubt all. You. Or a violet.

the progress

AND still we wear our uniforms, follow
The cracked cry of bugles, comb and brush
Our pride and prejudice, doctor the sallow
Initial ardor, wish to keep it fresh.
Still we applaud the President's voice and face.
Still we remark on patriotism, sing,
Salute the flag, thrill heavily, rejoice
For death of men who too saluted, sang.
But inward grows a soberness, an awe,
A fear, a deepening hollow through the cold.
For even if we come out standing up
How shall we smile, congratulate: and how
Settle in chairs? Listen, listen. The step
Of iron feet again. And again   wild.

The Bean Eaters

They eat beans mostly, this old yellow pair.
Dinner is a casual affair.
Plain chipware on a plain and creaking wood,
Tin flatware.

Two who are Mostly Good.
Two who have lived their day,
But keep on putting on their clothes
And putting things away.

And remembering . . .
Remembering, with twinklings and twinges,
As they lean over the beans in their rented back room that
      is full of beads and receipts and dolls and cloths,
      tobacco crumbs, vases and fringes.

We Real Cool

THE POOL PLAYERS.
SEVEN AT THE GOLDEN SHOVEL.

We real cool. We
Left school. We

Lurk late. We
Strike straight. We

Sing sin. We
Thin gin. We

Jazz June. We
Die soon.

The Lovers of the Poor

        arrive. The Ladies from the Ladies' Betterment League
Arrive in the afternoon, the late light slanting
In diluted gold bars across the boulevard brag
Of proud, seamed faces with mercy and murder hinting
Here, there, interrupting, all deep and debonair,
The pink paint on the innocence of fear;

Walk in a gingerly manner up the hall.
Cutting with knives served by their softest care,
Served by their love, so barbarously fair.
Whose mothers taught: You'd better not be cruel!
You had better not throw stones upon the wrens!
Herein they kiss and coddle and assault
Anew and dearly in the innocence
With which they baffle nature. Who are full,
Sleek, tender-clad, fit, fiftyish, a-glow, all
Sweetly abortive, hinting at fat fruit,
Judge it high time that fiftyish fingers felt
Beneath the lovelier planes of enterprise.
To resurrect. To moisten with milky chill.
To be a random hitching post or plush.
To be, for wet eyes, random and handy hem.
          Their guild is giving money to the poor.
The worthy poor. The very very worthy
And beautiful poor. Perhaps just not too swarthy?
Perhaps just not too dirty nor too dim
Nor—passionate. In truth, what they could wish
Is—something less than derelict or dull.
Not staunch enough to stab, though, gaze for gaze!
God shield them sharply from the beggar-bold!
The noxious needy ones whose battle's bald
Nonetheless for being voiceless, hits one down.

But it's all so bad! and entirely too much for them.
The stench; the urine, cabbage, and dead beans,
Dead porridges of assorted dusty grains,
The old smoke, *heavy* diapers, and, they're told,
Something called chitterlings. The darkness. Drawn
Darkness, or dirty light. The soil that stirs.
The soil that looks the soil of centuries.
And for that matter the *general* oldness. Old
Wood. Old marble. Old tile. Old old old.
Not homekind Oldness! Not Lake Forest, Glencoe.
Nothing is sturdy, nothing is majestic,
There is no quiet drama, no rubbed glaze, no
Unkillable infirmity of such
A tasteful turn as lately they have left,
Glencoe, Lake Forest, and to which their cars
Must presently restore them. When they're done
With dullards and distortions of this fistic
Patience of the poor and put-upon.
      They've never seen such a make-do-ness as
Newspaper rugs before! In this, this "flat,"
Their hostess is gathering up the oozed, the rich
Rugs of the morning (tattered! the bespattered . . .),
Readies to spread clean rugs for afternoon.
Here is a scene for you. The Ladies look,
In horror, behind a substantial citizeness
Whose trains clank out across her swollen heart.
Who, arms akimbo, almost fills a door.

All tumbling children, quilts dragged to the floor
And tortured thereover, potato peelings, soft-
Eyed kitten, hunched-up, haggard, to-be-hurt.
       Their League is allotting largesse to the Lost.
But to put their clean, their pretty money, to put
Their money collected from delicate rose-fingers
Tipped with their hundred flawless rose-nails seems . . .
       They own Spode, Lowestoft, candelabra,
Mantels, and hostess gowns, and sunburst clocks,
Turtle soup, Chippendale, red satin "hangings,"
Aubussons and Hattie Carnegie. They Winter
In Palm Beach; cross the Water in June; attend,
When suitable, the nice Art Institute;
Buy the right books in the best bindings; saunter
On Michigan, Easter mornings, in sun or wind.
Oh Squalor! This sick four-story hulk, this fibre
With fissures everywhere! Why, what are bringings
Of loathe-love largesse? What shall peril hungers
So old old, what shall flatter the desolate?
Tin can, blocked fire escape and chitterling
And swaggering seeking youth and the puzzled wreckage
Of the middle passage, and urine and stale shames
And, again, the porridges of the underslung
And children children children. Heavens! That
Was a rat, surely, off there, in the shadows? Long
And long-tailed? Gray? The Ladies from the Ladies'
Betterment League agree it will be better

To achieve the outer air that rights and steadies,
To hie to a house that does not holler, to ring
Bells elsetime, better presently to cater
To no more Possibilities, to get
Away. Perhaps the money can be posted.
Perhaps they two may choose another Slum!
Some serious sooty half-unhappy home!—
Where loathe-love likelier may be invested.
       Keeping their scented bodies in the center
Of the hall as they walk down the hysterical hall,
They allow their lovely skirts to graze no wall,
Are off at what they manage of a canter,
And, resuming all the clues of what they were,
Try to avoid inhaling the laden air.

The Ballad of Rudolph Reed

Rudolph Reed was oaken.
His wife was oaken too.
And his two good girls and his good little man
Oakened as they grew.

"I am not hungry for berries.
I am not hungry for bread.
But hungry hungry for a house
Where at night a man in bed

"May never hear the plaster
Stir as if in pain.
May never hear the roaches
Falling like fat rain.

"Where never wife and children need
Go blinking through the gloom.
Where every room of many rooms
Will be full of room.

"Oh my home may have its east or west
Or north or south behind it.
All I know is I shall know it,
And fight for it when I find it."

It was in a street of bitter white
That he made his application.
For Rudolph Reed was oakener
Than others in the nation.

The agent's steep and steady stare
Corroded to a grin.
Why, you black old, tough old hell of a man,
Move your family in!

Nary a grin grinned Rudolph Reed,
Nary a curse cursed he,
But moved in his House. With his dark little wife,
And his dark little children three.

A neighbor would *look*, with a yawning eye
That squeezed into a slit.
But the Rudolph Reeds and the children three
Were too joyous to notice it.

For were they not firm in a home of their own
With windows everywhere
And a beautiful banistered stair
And a front yard for flowers and a back yard for grass?

The first night, a rock, big as two fists.
The second, a rock big as three.
But nary a curse cursed Rudolph Reed.
(Though oaken as man could be.)

The third night, a silvery ring of glass.
Patience ached to endure.
But he looked, and lo! small Mabel's blood
Was staining her gaze so pure.

Then up did rise our Rudolph Reed
And pressed the hand of his wife,
And went to the door with a thirty-four
And a beastly butcher knife.

He ran like a mad thing into the night.
And the words in his mouth were stinking.
By the time he had hurt his first white man
He was no longer thinking.

By the time he had hurt his fourth white man
Rudolph Reed was dead.
His neighbors gathered and kicked his corpse.
"Nigger—" his neighbors said.

Small Mabel whimpered all night long,
For calling herself the cause.
Her oak-eyed mother did no thing
But change the bloody gauze.

Malcolm X
For Dudley Randall

Original.
Ragged-round.
Rich-robust.

He had the hawk-man's eyes.
We gasped. We saw the maleness.
The maleness raking out and making guttural the air
and pushing us to walls.

And in a soft and fundamental hour
a sorcery devout and vertical
beguiled the world.

He opened us—
who was a key,

who was a man.

Fire

from *The Third Sermon on the Warpland*

Phoenix

"In Egyptian mythology, a bird which lived for
five hundred years and then consumed itself in fire,
rising renewed from the ashes."

— Webster

Fire.
That is their way of lighting candles in the darkness.
A White Philosopher said
'It is better to light one candle than curse the darkness.'
These candles curse—
inverting the deeps of the darkness.

GUARD HERE, GUNS LOADED.
The young men run.
The children in ritual chatter
scatter upon
their Own and old geography.

The Law comes sirening across the town.

An Aspect of Love, Alive in the Ice and Fire
LaBohem Brown

It is the morning of our love.

In a package of minutes there is this We.
How beautiful.
Merry foreigners in our morning,
we laugh, we touch each other,
are responsible props and posts.

A physical light is in the room.

Because the world is at the window
we cannot wonder very long.

You rise. Although
genial, you are in yourself again.
I observe
your direct and respectable stride.
You are direct and self-accepting as a lion
in African velvet. You are level, lean,
remote.

These is a moment in Camaraderie
when interruption is not to be understood.
I cannot bear an interruption.

This is the shining joy;
the time of not-to-end.

On the street we smile.
We go
in different directions
down the imperturbable street.

The Life of Lincoln West

Ugliest little boy
that everyone ever saw.
That is what everyone said.

Even to his mother it was apparent—
when the blue-aproned nurse came into the
northeast end of the maternity ward
bearing his squeals and plump bottom
looped up in a scant receiving blanket,
bending, to pass the bundle carefully
into the waiting mother-hands—that this
was no cute little ugliness, no sly baby waywardness
that was going to inch away
as would baby fat, baby curl, and

baby spot-rash. The pendulous lip, the
branching ears, the eyes so wide and wild,
the vague unvibrant brown of the skin,
and, most disturbing, the great head.
These components of That Look bespoke
the sure fibre. The deep grain.

His father could not bear the sight of him.
His mother high-piled her pretty dyed hair and
put him among her hairpins and sweethearts,
dance slippers, torn paper roses.
He was not less than these,
he was not more.

As the little Lincoln grew,
uglily upward and out, he began
to understand that something was
wrong. His little ways of trying
to please his father, the bringing
of matches, the jumping aside at
warning sound of oh-so-large and
rushing stride, the smile that gave
and gave and gave—Unsuccessful!

Even Christmases and Easters were spoiled.
He would be sitting at the
family feasting table, really

delighting in the displays of mashed potatoes
and the rich golden
fat-crust of the ham or the festive
fowl, when he would look up and find
somebody feeling indignant about him.

What a pity what a pity. No love
for one so loving. The little Lincoln
loved Everybody. Ants. The changing
caterpillar. His much-missing mother.
His kindergarten teacher.

His kindergarten teacher—whose
concern for him was composed of one
part sympathy and two parts repulsion.
The others ran up with their little drawings.
He ran up with his.
She
tried to be as pleasant with him as
with others, but it was difficult.
For she was all pretty! all daintiness,
all tiny vanilla, with blue eyes and fluffy
sun-hair. One afternoon she
saw him in the hall looking bleak against
the wall. It was strange because the
bell had long since rung and no other
child was in sight. Pity flooded her.
She buttoned her gloves and suggested

cheerfully that she walk him home. She
started out bravely, holding him by the
hand. But she had not walked far before
she regretted it. The little monkey.
Must everyone look? And clutching her
hand like that . . . Literally pinching
it . . .

At seven, the little Lincoln loved
the brother and sister who
moved next door. Handsome. Well-
dressed. Charitable, often, to him. They
enjoyed him because he was
resourceful, made up
games, told stories. But when
their More Acceptable friends came they turned
their handsome backs on him. He
hated himself for his feeling
of well-being when with them despite—
Everything.

He spent much time looking at himself
in mirrors. What could be done?
But there was no
shrinking his head. There was no
binding his ears.

"Don't touch me!" cried the little
fairy-like being in the playground.

Her name was Nerissa. The many
children were playing tag, but when
he caught her, she recoiled, jerked free
and ran. It was like all the
rainbow that ever was, going off
forever, all, all the sparklings in
the sunset west.

One day, while he was yet seven,
a thing happened. In the down-town movies
with his mother a white
man in the seat beside him whispered
loudly to a companion, and pointed at
the little Linc.
"THERE! That's the kind I've been wanting
to show you! One of the best
examples of the specie. Not like
those diluted Negroes you see so much of on
the streets these days, but the
real thing.

Black, ugly, and odd. You
can see the savagery. The blunt
blankness. That is the real
thing."

His mother—her hair had never looked so
red around the dark brown
velvet of her face—jumped up,
shrieked "Go to—" She did not finish.
She yanked to his feet the little
Lincoln, who was sitting there
staring in fascination at his assessor. At the author of his
new idea.

All the way home he was happy. Of course,
he had not liked the word
"ugly."
But, after, should he not
be used to that by now? What had
struck him, among words and meanings
he could little understand, was the phrase
"the real thing."
He didn't know quite why,
but he liked that.
He liked that very much.

When he was hurt, too much
stared at—
too much
left alone—he
thought about that. He told himself
"After all, I'm
the real thing."

It comforted him.

To Don at Salaam

I like to see you lean back in your chair
so far you have to fall but do not—
your arms back, your fine hands
in your print pockets.

Beautiful. Impudent.
Ready for life.
A tied storm.

I like to see you wearing your boy smile
whose tribute is for two of us or three.

Sometimes in life
things seem to be moving
and they are not
and they are not
there.
You are there.

Your voice is the listened-for music.
Your act is the consolidation.

I like to see you living in the world.

Paul Robeson

That time
we all heard it,
cool and clear,
cutting across the hot grit of the day.
The major Voice.
The adult Voice
forgoing Rolling River,
forgoing tearful tale of bale and barge
and other symptoms of an old despond.
Warning, in music-words
devout and large,
that we are each other's
harvest:
we are each other's
business:
we are each other's
magnitude and bond.

The Boy Died in My Alley

to Running Boy

The Boy died in my alley
without my Having Known.
Policeman said, next morning,
"Apparently died Alone."

"You heard a shot?" Policeman said.
Shots I hear and Shots I hear.
I never see the Dead.

The Shot that killed him yes I heard
as I heard the Thousand shots before;
careening tinnily down the nights
across my years and arteries.

Policeman pounded on my door.
"Who is it?" "POLICE!" Policeman yelled.
"A Boy was dying in your alley.
A Boy is dead, and in your alley.
And have you known this Boy before?"

I have known this Boy before.
I have known this Boy before, who
ornaments my alley.

I never saw his face at all.
I never saw his futurefall.
But I have known this Boy.

I have always heard him deal with death.
I have always heard the shout, the volley.
I have closed my heart-ears late and early.
And I have killed him ever.

I joined the Wild and killed him
with knowledgeable unknowing.
I saw where he was going.
I saw him Crossed. And seeing,
I did not take him down.

He cried not only "Father!"
but "Mother!
Sister!
Brother."
The cry climbed up the alley.
It went up to the wind.
It hung upon the heaven
for a long
stretch-strain of Moment.

The red floor of my alley
is a special speech to me.

Elegy In a Rainbow

Moe Belle's double love song

When I was a little girl
   Christmas was exquisite.
   I didn't touch it.
I didn't look at it too closely.
   To do that to do that
might nullify the shine.

Thus with a Love
that has to have a Home
like the Black Nation,
like the Black Nation
defining its own Roof
that no one else can see.

A Black Wedding Song

First dedicated to Charles and La Tanya,
Allen and Glenda, Haki and Safisha.

I

This love is a rich cry over
the deviltries and the death.
A weapon-song. Keep it strong.

Keep it strong.
Keep it logic and Magic and lightning and Muscle.

Strong hand in strong hand, stride to
the Assault that is promised you (knowing
no armor assaults a pudding or a mush.)

Here is your Wedding Day.
Here is your launch.

Come to your Wedding Song.

II

For you
I wish the kindness that romps or sorrows along.
Or kneels.

I wish you the daily forgiveness of each other.
For war comes in from the World
and puzzles a darling duet—
tangles tongues,
tears hearts, mashes minds;
there will be the need to forgive.

I wish you jewels of black love.

Come to your Wedding Song.

Horses Graze

Cows graze.
Horses graze.
They
eat
eat
eat.
Their graceful heads
are bowed
bowed
bowed
in majestic oblivion.
They are nobly oblivious
to your follies,

your inflation,
the knocks and nettles of administration.
They
eat
eat
eat.
And at the crest of their brute satisfaction,
with wonderful gentleness, in affirmation,
they lift their clean calm eyes and they lie down
and love the world.
They speak with their companions.
They do not wish that they were otherwhere.
Perhaps they know that creature feet may press
only a few earth inches at a time,
that earth is anywhere earth,
that an eye may see,
wherever it may be,
the Immediate arc, alone, of life, of love.

In Sweden,
China,
Afrika,
in India or Maine
the animals are sane;
they know and know and know
there's ground below
and sky
up high.

"When Handed a Lemon, Make Lemonade"
(title by Anonymous)

I've lived through lemons,
sugaring them.
"When handed a lemon,
make lemonade."
That is what
some sage has said.
"When handed a lemon,
make lemonade."

There is always a use
for lemon juice.

Do you know what to do with
trouble, children?
Make lemonade. Make lemonade.
"Handed a lemon, make lemonade."

Friend

Walking with you
shuts off shivering.
Here we are.
Here we are.

I am with you to share and to bear and to care.

This is warm.
I want you happy, I want you warm.

Your Friend for our forever is what I am.
Your Friend in thorough thankfulness.

It is the evening of our love.
Evening is hale and whole.
Evening shall not go out.
Evening is comforting flame.
Evening is comforting flame.

Sources

Brooks, Gwendolyn. *A Street in Bronzeville*. New York: Harper, 1945.

kitchenette building
when you have forgotten Sunday: the love story
love note I: surely
the progress

Brooks, Gwendolyn. *The Bean Eaters*. New York: Harper, 1960.

The Bean Eaters
We Real Cool
The Lovers of the Poor
The Ballad of Rudolph Reed

Brooks, Gwendolyn. *In the Mecca*. New York: Harper, 1968.

Malcolm X

Brooks, Gwendolyn. *Riot*. Detroit: Broadside Press, 1969.

Fire, from The Third Sermon on the Warpland
An Aspect of Love, Alive in the Ice and Fire

Brooks, Gwendolyn. *Family Pictures*. Detroit: Broadside, 1970.

> The Life of Lincoln West
> To Don at Salaam
> Paul Robeson

Brooks, Gwendolyn. *Beckonings*. Detroit: Broadside, 1975.

> The Boy Died in My Alley
> Elegy In a Rainbow
> A Black Wedding Song
> Horses Graze
> "When Handed a Lemon, Make Lemonade"
> Friend

etheridge knight

Etheridge Knight
Albert M. Ward

> Gone   Gone
> Another weaver of black dreams has gone
>
> ("For Langston Hughes" 1-2)

"Ba' Brother . . ."

When I met Etheridge Knight, I thought of my uncles in St. Louis, Missouri. His presence felt so familiar. I thought of the old guys who taught me to play checkers when I was a kid at Hank's Barbershop on Linwood in Detroit. You know them. They tell stories, sit on stoops, haunt doorways, appear from nowhere, and speak uncomfortable truths. They school young 'uns about playing the game and dealing with the Man. They taught me well.

I had always admired my St. Louis uncles, my mother's brothers, and their people-wise ways. My grandmother would tell me that I reminded her especially of my uncle Billy, her youngest son. I would smile thinking, if only I could be that black and that bad. There was something about my uncles' eyes that Etheridge describes in one of his poems:

> He sees through stone
> He has the secret
> eyes . . .
>
> ("He Sees Through Stone" 1-3)

I would often wonder: at what cost comes a life with eyes that could see through stone? I can feel that cost in Etheridge's poetry.

Etheridge Knight was born on April 19, 1931 in Mississippi in a place called Corinth. I think of Corinth as a city of ancient Greece where the temples of Apollo and Aphrodite were located. How interesting that the muses of antiquity might come to rest in Mississippi with a black man as a modern day oracle. Etheridge dropped out of school before he was seventeen and joined the Army. He was wounded in Korea and became addicted to drugs. As the Civil Rights and Black Power movements were beginning to transform communities across America, Etheridge was in prison for robbery under an eight-year sentence. While in prison, Etheridge was encouraged by Gwendolyn Brooks and Dudley Randall to write. He wrote poems, often about his experience of incarceration, which later became his first book, *Poems From Prison,* published in 1968 by Broadside Press. On the back cover of the original edition of *Poems from Prison*, Etheridge describes poetry as a life-giving soul-saving force: *"I died in Korea from a shrapnel wound and narcotics resurrected me. I died in 1960 from a prison sentence and poetry brought me back to life."*

Etheridge Knight's work speaks to the lives of so many men, lost and found. You can feel his struggle to survive an environment that was devouring his humanity. You can hear his wounding, anger, and passion give voice to his words and power to his poetry. You can hear his voice like an acoustic guitar—sweet, steely, guttural, and edged. Etheridge found freedom and dignity through his poetry and perhaps, most of all, a second chance.

Etheridge's conversation is for "grown folks." He is not timid about his origin or his roots:

> I was born in Mississippi;
> I walked barefooted thru the mud.
> Born black in Mississippi,
> Walked barefooted thru the mud.
> But, when I reached the age of twelve
> I left that place for good. (1-6)

These lines open his poem, "A Poem for Myself (Or Blues for a Mississippi Black Boy)," where Etheridge makes it very clear that he is a man of no pretense. For Etheridge, life is not some aesthetically romantic and ideal promenade, but more something that oozes and squishes between the toes. As today's young poets might say of Knight's work: "he's about keepin' it real." His audience is forced to *deal* with his work and, therefore, deal with him.

As a black poet, I am confronted by his work to acknowledge him as kinsman. In his poem, "For Black Poets Who Think of Suicide," he issues us this challenge: "Let All Black Poets die as trumpets" (12). In Etheridge's view, black poets belong to their community. It is their duty to live and stand as heralds giving point and voice to the struggle of black people to thrive and be free in a culture and society that too often has exploited, excluded, or denied their humanity and contributions to the world. The words of black poets must call to action the determination and strength of the black community to fight oppression and discrimination by and within the greater society. Moreover, poets must strive to create possibilities for our families and children to live fruitful and meaning-filled lives.

Etheridge wept poetry. When he speaks of his isolation from his family, the loss of his beloved, and the streets he walked alone; when he speaks of his loss of freedom and sense of place, I hear the pitch and wail of Africans torn from their ancestral homes and constellations. I know, as my uncles would know, as the old men who taught me to play checkers would know these lines in Knight's poem "Belly Song":

> And this poem
> this poem/is/for ME—for me
> and the days/that lay/in the back/of my mind
> when the sea/rose up/
>   to swallow me
> and the streets I walked
>   were lonely streets
>   were stone/cold streets

```
this poem
this poem/is/
for me/and the nights
        when I
wrapped my feelings
        in a sheet of ice
and stared
        at the stars
            thru iron bars
            and cried
in the middle of my eyes. . . . (53-71)
```

In a 1967 article written for the *Liberator* entitled "Black Writing is Socio-Creative Art," Charles Fuller, Jr. asserts: "Socio-creative art is what Black men bring into existence when they sit down to write—indeed it corresponds directly, *for us*, to the meaning of art. Our lives and our art are one in the same struggle. . . . " (9). Poetry for Etheridge Knight became his art of living. Truth or dare, Etheridge Knight speaks out loud in his work of his existence as a Black man with no apologies. His truth is that he lived in a world that would deny him his rights to his self, his ancestors, and his community. He survived prison, war, heartbreak, and lost dreams. He dares you to look at him and not see his humanity. His poetry is his testimony.

I really would have liked to have played checkers, dominoes, perhaps even horseshoes with Etheridge. Or, walked around Belle Isle, watched the boats, and talked with the folks fishing off of the Detroit River. I would have listened to him and learned from his stories about life, poetry, black men. I would have told him about my St. Louis uncles . . . and how much he reminded me of them.

Perhaps we would have talked of love, community, loneliness, and women. Perhaps we might have shared poems about ancestry and revolutionary visions. Perhaps, he would have chosen *to school this young 'un*.

I once had the opportunity to read with Etheridge at a poetry event in Detroit sponsored by Broadside Press. I was really nervous. Actually, I wanted to go sit in the audience and just listen as he did his thing. I was sitting right next to him. My reading was a little shaky and edgy. It certainly wasn't one of my best. I wasn't yet quite used to reading so publicly. I will always remember what Etheridge said to me when I returned to my chair beside him:

> *"Me too . . . I'm afraid every time. . . ."*

Then, it was his turn.

I have had the privilege of traveling to Indianapolis to the annual Etheridge Knight Poetry Festival and meeting some of his family. When I was there the Last Poets were being featured. His hometown seemed so familiar, then I remembered. We would come this way, my folks, me, my sister on our way to St. Louis from Detroit to see Big Momma, my grandmother, and her sons . . . my uncles . . . my kin. . . .

> *Ladies and Gentlemen, Brothers, Sisters, friends—*
> *It is my privilege to introduce to some and present to others,*
> *the words and poetry of Mr. Etheridge Knight.*

Gone   Gone
Another weaver of black dreams has gone

Works Cited

Fuller, Charles H., Jr. "Black Writing is Socio-Creative Art." *Liberator* 7.4 (April 1967): 8-10.

Hard Rock Returns to Prison from the Hospital for the Criminal Insane

Hard Rock was "known not to take no shit
From nobody," and he had the scars to prove it:
Split purple lips, lumped ears, welts above
His yellow eyes, and one long scar that cut
Across his temple and plowed through a thick
Canopy of kinky hair.

The WORD was that Hard Rock wasn't a mean nigger
Anymore, that the doctors had bored a hole in his head,
Cut out part of his brain, and shot electricity
Through the rest. When they brought Hard Rock back,
Handcuffed and chained, he was turned loose,
Like a freshly gelded stallion, to try his new status.
And we all waited and watched, like indians at a corral,
To see if the WORD was true.

As we waited we wrapped ourselves in the cloak
Of his exploits: "Man, the last time, it took eight
Screws to put him in the Hole." "Yeah, remember when he
Smacked the captain with his dinner tray?" "He set
The record for time in the Hole—67 straight days!"
"Ol Hard Rock! man, that's one crazy nigger."
And then the jewel of a myth that Hard Rock had once bit
A screw on the thumb and poisoned him with syphilitic spit.

The testing came, to see if Hard Rock was really tame.
A hillbilly called him a black son of a bitch
And didn't lose his teeth, a screw who knew Hard Rock
From before shook him down and barked in his face.
And Hard Rock did *nothing*. Just grinned and looked silly,
His eyes empty like knot holes in a fence.

And even after we discovered that it took Hard Rock
Exactly 3 minutes to tell you his first name,
We told ourselves that he had just wised up,
Was being cool; but we could not fool ourselves for long,
And we turned away, our eyes on the ground. Crushed.
He had been our Destroyer, the doer of things
We dreamed of doing but could not bring ourselves to do,
The fears of years, like a biting whip,
Had cut grooves too deeply across our backs.

He Sees Through Stone

He sees through stone
he has the secret
eyes this old black one
who under prison skies
sits pressed by the sun

against the western wall
his pipe between purple gums

the years fall
like overripe plums
bursting red flesh
on the dark earth

his time is not my time
but I have known him
in a time gone

he led me trembling cold
into the dark forest
taught me the secret rites
to take a woman
to be true to my brothers
to make my spear drink
the blood
of my enemies

now black cats circle him
flash white teeth
snarl at the air
mashing green grass beneath
shining muscles
ears peeling his words

he smiles
he knows
the hunt   the enemy
he has the secret eyes
he sees through stone

The Idea of Ancestry

1

Taped to the wall of my cell are 47 pictures: 47 black
faces: my father, mother, grandmothers (1 dead), grand
fathers (both dead), brothers, sisters, uncles, aunts,
cousins (1st & 2nd), nieces, and nephews. They stare
across the space at me sprawling on my bunk. I know
their dark eyes, they know mine. I know their style,
they know mine. I am all of them, they are all of me;
they are farmers, I am a thief, I am me, they are thee.

I have at one time or another been in love with my mother,
1 grandmother, 2 sisters, 2 aunts (1 went to the asylum),
and 5 cousins. I am now in love with a 7 yr old niece
(she sends me letters in large block print, and
her picture is the only one that smiles at me).

I have the same name as 1 grandfather, 3 cousins, 3 nephews,
and 1 uncle. The uncle disappeared when he was 15, just took
off and caught a freight (they say). He's discussed each year
when the family has a reunion, he causes uneasiness in
the clan, he is an empty space. My father's mother, who is 93
and who keeps the Family Bible with everybody's birth dates
(and death dates) in it, always mentions him. There is no
place in her Bible for "whereabouts unknown."

2

Each fall the graves of my grandfathers call me, the brown
hills and red gullies of mississippi send out their electric
messages, galvanizing my genes. Last yr/like a salmon quitting
the cold ocean—leaping and bucking up his birth stream/I
hitchhiked my way from L.A. with 16 caps in my pocket and a
monkey on my back. and I almost kicked it with the kinfolks.
I walked barefooted in my grandmother's backyard/I smelled the old
land and the woods/I sipped cornwhiskey from fruit jars with the men/
I flirted with the women/I had a ball till the caps ran out
and my habit came down. That night I looked at my grandmother
and split/my guts were screaming for junk/but I was almost
contented/I had almost caught up with me.
(The next day in Memphis I cracked a croaker's crib for a fix.)

This yr there is a gray stone wall damming my stream, and when the falling leaves stir my genes, I pace my cell or flop on my bunk and stare at 47 black faces across the space. I am all of them, they are all of me, I am me, they are thee, and I have no sons to float in the space between.

Haiku

1
Eastern guard tower
glints in sunset; convicts rest
like lizards on rocks.

2
The piano man
is sting at 3 am
his songs drop like plum.

3
Morning sun slants cell.
Drunks stagger like cripple flies
On Jailhouse floor.

4

To write a blues song
is to regiment riots
and pluck gems from graves.

5

A bare pecan tree
slips a pencil shadow down
a moonlit snow slope.

6

The falling snow flakes
Can not blunt the hard aches nor
Match the steel stillness.

7

Under moon shadows
A tall boy flashes knife and
Slices star bright ice.

8

In the August grass
Struck by the last rays of sun
The cracked teacup screams.

9

Making jazz swing in
Seventeen syllables AIN'T
No square poet's job.

To Make a Poem in Prison

It is hard
To make a poem in prison.
The air lends itself not
to the singer.
The seasons creep by unseen
And spark no fresh fires.

Soft words are rare, and drunk drunk
Against the clang of keys;
Wide eyes stare fat zeros
And plea only for pity.

Pity is not for the poet;
Yet poems must be primed.
Here is not even sadness for singing,
Not even a beautiful rage rage,
No birds are winging. The air
Is empty of laughter. And love?
Why, love has flown,
Love has gone to glitten.

As You Leave Me

Shiny record albums scattered over
the livingroom floor, reflecting light
from the lamp, sharp reflections that hurt
my eyes as I watch you, squatting among the platters,
the beer foam making mustaches on your lips.

And, too,
the shadows on your cheeks from your long lashes
fascinate me—almost as much as the dimples:
in your cheeks, your arms and your legs:
dimples . . . dimples . . . dimples . . .

You
hum along with Mathis—how you love Mathis!
with his burnished hair and quicksilver voice that dances
among the stars and whirls through canyons
like windblown snow. sometimes I think that Mathis
could take you from me if you could be complete
without me. I glance at my watch. it is now time.

You rise,
silently, and to the bedroom and the paint:
on the lips red, on the eyes black,
and I lean in the doorway and smoke, and see you
grow old before my eyes, and smoke. why do you

chatter while you dress, and smile when you grab
your large leather purse? don't you know that when you
leave me I walk to the window and watch you? and light
a reefer as I watch you? and I die as I watch you
disappear in the dark streets
to whistle and to smile at the johns.

Portrait of Malcolm X
(For Charles Baker)

He has the sign
of the time shining
in his eyes   the high sign

His throat moans
Moses on Sinai and cracks
stones

His lips lay full and flowered
by the breast of Mother Africa

His forehead is red
and sacrosanct and
smooth as time and
love for you

To Dinah Washington

I have heard your voice floating, royal and real,
Across the dusky neighborhoods,
And the eyes of old men grow bright, remembering;
Children stop their play to listen,
Remembering—though they have never heard you before,
You are familiar to them:
Queen of the Blues, singing an eternal song.

In the scarred booths of Forty-Third street,
"Long Johns" suck in their bellies,
On the brass studded leather of Elite-town,
Silk-suited Bucks raise their chins . . .

Wherever a man is without a warm woman,
Or a woman without her muscled man,
The eternal song is sung.

Some say you're sleeping,
But I say you're singing.

Unforgettable Queen.

For Langston Hughes

Gone   Gone
   Another weaver of black dreams has gone
we sat in June Bug's pad with the shades drawn
and the air thick with holy smoke. and we heard
the Lady sing Langston before we knew his name.
and when Black Bodies stopped swinging   June
Bug, TG and I went out and swung on some white cats.
now I don't think the Mythmaker meant for us to do *that*
but we didn't know what else to do.

Gone   Gone
   Another weaver of black dreams has gone

To Gwendolyn Brooks

O Courier on Pegasus. O Daughter of Parnassus!
O Splendid woman of the purple stich.

When beaten and blue, despairingly we sink
Within obfuscating mire,
Oh, cradle in your bosom us, hum your lullabies
And soothe our souls with kisses of verse
That stir us on to search for light.

O Mother of the world. Effulgent lover of the Sun!
Forever speak the truth.

Apology for Apostasy?

Soft songs, like birds, die in poison air
So my song cannot now be candy.
Anger rots the oak and elm; roses are rare,
Seldom seen through blind despair.

And my murmur cannot be heard
Above the din and damn. The night is full
Of buggers and bastards; no moon or stars
Light the sky. And my candy is deferred

Till peacetime, when my voice shall be light,
Like down, lilting in the air; then shall I
Sing of beaches, white in the magic sun,
And of moons and maidens at midnight.

Genesis

the skin
of my poems
may be green. yes,
and sometimes
wrinkled
or worn

the snake shape
of my song
may cause
the heel
of Adam & Eve
to bleed. . . .

split my skin
with the rock
of love old
as the rock
of Moses
my poems
love you

Another Poem for Me
(after recovering from an O.D.)

what now
what now dumb nigger damn near dead
what now
now that you won't dance
behind the pale white doors of death
what now   is   to be
to be what you wanna be

what you spozed to be
or what white/america wants you to be
a lame crawling from nickel bag to nickel bag
be black brother/man be black
and blooming in the night
be black like your fat brother
sweating and straining to hold you
as you struggle against the straps
be black   be black like
your woman   her pained face floating
above you   her hands sliding
                under the sheets
to take yours   be black like
your mama sitting in a quiet corner
praying to a white/jesus to save her black boy

what now dumb nigger damn near dead
where is the correctness
the proper posture
the serious love of living
now that death has fled these quiet corridors

Relaxing in the Charity Ward at Mercy Hospital

All the old/men
                      lie dying
squirming in their own shit
in the Hospital named Mercy

All the old/men
                      lie dying
                      all day dying
                      in the morning dying

When the well/fed/pink cheeked priest
at break of day follows a white/starched nun
thru the Charity/Welfare ward at the Hospital
named Mercy. The fat well fed priest
B
l
e
ss all the old/men who
                      lie dying
squirming in their own shit

A Poem to Be Recited

A poem
to be recited
while waiting in line to sign/up for your unemployment check
or
while standing in line to be fed in the prison mess-hall
or
while boarding a troop/ship for Vietnam
or
while walking thru the playground in "the projects":

The Children in Blk america grow up quickly
(and they die young.
The Children in Blk america grow up quickly
(and they die young.

The Children in Blk america have sad eyes.
The Children in Blk america have sad eyes.
The Children of Blk america are ashamed of their fathers.
The children of Blk america are ashamed of their fathers.

No Moon Floods the Memory of That Night

No moon floods the memory of that night
only the rain I remember the cold rain
against our faces and mixing with your tears
only the rain I remember the cold rain
and your mouth soft and warm
no moon no stars no jagged pain
of lightning only my impotent tongue
and the red rage within my brain
knowing that the chilling rain was our forever
even as I tried to explain:

"A revolutionary is a doomed man
with no certainties but love and history."
"But our children must grow up with certainties
and they will make the revolution."
"By example we must show the way so plain
that our children can go neither right
nor left but straight to freedom."
"No," you said. And you left.

No moon floods the memory of that night
only the rain I remember the cold rain
and praying that like the falling water
returns to the sky you would return to me again.

Belly Song
(for the Daytop Family)

"You have made something
Out of the sea that blew
And rolled you on its salt bitter lips.
It nearly swallowed you.
But I hear
You are tough and harder to swallow than most. . . ."

—S. Mansfield

1

And I   and I/must admit
that the sea in you
            has sung/to the sea/in me
and I   and I/must admit
that the sea in me
            has fallen/in love
            with the sea in you
because you have made something
out of the sea
            that nearly swallowed you

And this poem
this poem
this poem/I give/to you.

this poem is a song/I sing/to you
from the bottom
      of the sea
          in my belly

this poem
this poem/is a song/about FEELINGS
about the Bone of feeling
about the Stone of feeling
      and the Feather of feeling

2

This poem/is/
a death/chant
and a grave/stone
and a prayer for the dead:
      for young Jackie Robinson.
a moving Blk/warrior who walked
among us
      with a wide/stride—and heavy heels
moving   moving   moving
thru the blood and mud and shit of Vietnam
moving   moving   moving
thru the blood and mud and dope of America
      for Jackie/who was/

a song
and a stone
and a Feather of feeling
      now dead
and/gone/in this month of love

this poem
this poem/is/a silver feather
and the sun-gold/glinting/green hills breathing
river flowing—for Sheryl and David—and
their first/ kiss by the river—for Mark and Sue
and a Sunday walk on her grand/father's farm
for Sammy and Marion—love/rhythms
for Michael and Jean—love/rhythms
love/rhythms—love/ rhythms—and LIFE.
for Karen J. and James D. and Roland M. and David P.
      who have not felt
the sun of their eighteenth summer. . . .

      3

And this poem
this poem/is/for ME—for me
and the days/that lay/in the back/of my mind
when the sea/rose up/
      to swallow me
and the streets I walked

were lonely streets
were stone/cold streets

this poem
this poem/is/
for me/and the nights
      when I
wrapped my feelings
      in a sheet of ice
and stared
    at the stars
        thru iron bars
          and cried
in the middle of my eyes. . . .

this poem
this poem
this poem/is/for me
     and my woman
     and the yesterdays
when she opened
      to me like a flower
but I fell on her
      like a stone
I fell on her like a stone. . . .

4

And now—in my 40th year
        I have come here
to this House of Feelings
to this Singing Sea
and I   and I/must admit
that the sea in me
        has fallen/in love
with the sea in you
because the sea
that now sings/in you
        is the same sea
that nearly swallowed you—
        and me too.

This Poem

This poem is for you
This poem is to inform you
This poem is for you to listen to
who you are/where you at/
This poem is to pull your coat to who
your enemy is and where he's at.
This poem is for all the Black Mothers, wet eyed and weary

watching their children die young, cut down by white america
like young roses broken in a hailstorm
This poem is for all the black Brothers dead and
dying in Vietnam, when they should be marching the
streets of Birmingham
This poem is for you, to comfort you
This poem/is/to help you out of bed when the morning is
cold and the day's work is hard. This poem is to soothe you
when your woman is gone and you're all alone,
This poem is to help you to be a man Now, to move to
Freedom Now,—
This poem is for the junkies nodding on 125th St.
This poem is for the whores walking on Beale St.
This poem is for the brothers in foundries at Ford,
Chrysler, and General Motors.
This poem is for the sisters typing, nursing, cooking,
teaching, and standing on assembly lines.
This poem is a love poem to you.

For Black Poets Who Think of Suicide

Black Poets should live—not leap
From steel bridges (Like the white boys do.
Black Poets should *live*—not lay
Their necks on railroad tracks (like the white boys do.
Black Poets should seek—but not search too much
In sweet dark caves, nor hunt for snipe
Down psychic trails (like the white boys do.

For Black Poets belong to Black People. Are
The Flutes of Black Lovers. Are
The Organs of Black Sorrows. Are
The Trumpets of Black Warriors.
Let All Black Poets die as trumpets,
And be buried in the dust of marching feet.

Jazz Drummer

MAX ROACH
    has fire and steel in his hands,
    rides high, is a Makabele warrior,
    tastes death on his lips, beats babies
    from worn out wombs,
                grins with grace,
    and cries in the middle of his eyes.

MAX ROACH
    thumps the big circle in bare feet,
    opens wide the big arms,
    and like the sea
            calls us all.

A Poem for Myself
(Or Blues for a Mississippi Black Boy)

I was born in Mississippi;
I walked barefooted thru the mud.
Born black in Mississippi,
Walked barefooted thru the mud.
But, when I reached the age of twelve
I left that place for good.
My daddy he chopped cotton
And he drank his liquor straight.
Said my daddy chopped cotton
And he drank his liquor straight.
When I left that Sunday morning
He was leaning on the barnyard gate.
I left my momma standing
With the sun shining in her eyes.
Left her standing in the yard
With the sun shining in her eyes.
And I headed North

As straight as the Wild Goose Flies,
I been to Detroit & Chicago—
Been to New York city too.
I been to Detroit and Chicago
Been to New York city too.
Said I done strolled all those funky avenues
I'm still the same old black boy with the same old blues.
Going back to Mississippi
This time to stay for good
Going back to Mississippi
This time to stay for good—
Gonna be free in Mississippi
Or dead in the Mississippi mud.

The Bones of My Father

There are no dry bones
here in this valley. The skull
of my father grins
at the Mississippi moon
from the bottom
of the Tallahatchie,
the bones of my father
are buried in the mud
of these creeks and brooks that twist

and flow their secrets to the sea.
but the wind sings to me
here the sun speaks to me
of the dry bones of my father.

2

There are no dry bones
in the northern valley, in the Harlem alleys
young/black/men with knees bent
nod on the stoops of the tenements
and dream
of the dry bones of my father.

And young white longhairs who flee
their homes, and bend their minds
and sing their songs of brotherhood
and no more wars are searching for
my father's bones.

3

There are no dry bones
here, my brothers. We hide from the sun.
No more do we take the long straight strides.
Our steps have been shaped by the cages
that kept us. We glide sideways

like crabs across the sand.
We perch on green lilies, we search
beneath white rocks. . . .
THERE ARE NO DRY BONES HERE

The skull of my father
grins at the Mississippi moon
from the bottom
of the Tallahatchie.

Cop-out Session

I done shot dope, been to jail, swilled
wine, ripped off sisters, passed bad checks,
changed my name, howled at the moon,
wrote poems, turned
backover flips, flipped over backwards,
(in other words)
I been confused, fucked up, scared, phony
and jive
to a whole/lot of people . . .

Haven't you?
                        In one way or another?

Enybody else wanna cop-out?

Sources

Knight, Etheridge. *Poems from Prison*. Detroit: Broadside Press, 1968.

Hard Rock Returns to Prison from the Hospital for the Criminal Insane
He Sees through Stone
The Idea of Ancestry
Haiku
To Make a Poem in Prison
As You Leave Me
Portrait of Malcolm X
To Dinah Washington
For Langston Hughes
To Gwendolyn Brooks
Apology for Apostasy?

Knight, Etheridge. *Belly Song and Other Poems*. Detroit: Broadside Press, 1973.

Genesis
Another Poem for Me
Relaxing in the Charity Ward at Mercy Hospital
A Poem to be Recited
No Moon Floods the Memory of That Night
Belly Song
This Poem
For Black Poets Who Think of Suicide
Jazz Drummer
A Poem for Myself
The Bones of My Father
Cop-out Session

JEB (Joan E. Biren) © 2004 and the Audre Lorde Collection, Spelman College Archives

audre lorde

Audre Lorde: Brave Words of a Warrior Woman
Willie Williams

Audre Lorde frequently described herself as a "black, feminist, lesbian, mother, poet warrior." Her work and her life were dedicated to exploring and integrating these complex aspects of herself. As Nancy K. Bereano writes in the introduction to Lorde's seminal collection of essays, *Sister Outsider: Essays and Speeches by Audre Lorde* (1984): "Audre Lorde's writing is an impulse to wholeness. . . . Out of her desire for wholeness, her need to encompass and address all the parts of herself, she teaches us about the significance of *difference*—'that raw and powerful connection from which our personal power is forged'" (8). In refusing to silence any aspect of her identity, Lorde taught others how to connect to their own power and each other.

Audrey Geraldine Lorde was born on February 18, 1934 in Harlem, New York of Grenadian immigrant parents. She was attracted to literature and language from a very young age: "Words had an energy and power and I came to respect that power early. Pronouns, nouns, and verbs were citizens of different countries, who really got together to make a new world" (Hammond 20). A voracious reader, Lorde began writing her own poetry in eighth grade. She had her first publication while in high school. By her teens she also had begun what would be a life-long habit of self-examination, which she carried out through the practice of journaling. From these journals she would later fashion much of her poetry.

Lorde received her BA degree in philosophy and English from Hunter College and a Master of Library Sciences degree from Columbia University. In the 1960s her poems appeared in a number of periodicals and anthologies, including *Journal of Black Poetry*, *Negro Digest*, *Venture*, and *New Negro Poets* (1964) edited by Langston Hughes. Her first book of poetry, *The First Cities*, was published in 1968 (De Veaux).

Lorde's relationship with Broadside Press began when Dudley Randall agreed to distribute her second book, *Cables to Rage* (1970), published by Paul Bremen Press in England. Broadside Press then published *From a Land Where Other People Live* in 1973, which was nominated for The National Book award for that year, and *New York Head Shop and Museum* in 1974.

For Lorde, poetry was not only an aesthetic pursuit; it was a necessary, powerful, and life-giving force:

> . . . it is through poetry that we give name to those ideas which are—until the poem—nameless and formless, about to be birthed, but already felt. . . . For women, then, poetry is not a luxury. It is a vital necessity of our existence. It forms the quality of the light within which we predicate our hopes and dreams toward survival and change, first made into language, then into idea, then into more tangible action. . . . Poetry is not only dream and vision; it is the skeleton architecture of our lives. ("Poetry Is Not a Luxury" 36-8)

When we read a Lorde poem, we feel the poet's intense engagement with ideas. The poems work on multiple levels, with many ideas being explored at once. We sense the poet's unwavering intention to achieve clarity and resolution. For all of its conceptual density, however, the language of her poetry is remarkably lean. Her images, often drawn from everyday life, are infused with an emotional intensity. The connections the images embody are frequently surprising and revealing of the complexity of daily experience. In many of Lorde's poems, there is a persona who is urging us to think along, teaching us, revealing to us the sometimes painful, sometimes life-affirming truths hidden before our very eyes.

Lorde played a major role in both the Black Arts and the Civil Rights movements of the sixties and seventies, not only as a poet, but as an activist, teacher, and innovator of Black Studies programs in traditionally Black colleges of the South and in northern universities. The extent of her commitment to activism is reflected in many of her early poems. She is concerned with both the specifics of the African American struggle and with the oppression of peoples world-wide. In the poem "Equinox," we see her making connections between her concerns for her own family and her consciousness of the suffering of those caught up in wars across the globe:

> The year my daughter was born
> DuBois died in Accra while I
> marched into Washington
> to a death knell of dreaming
> which 250,000 others mistook for a hope

believing only Birmingham's black children
were being pounded into mortar in churches
that year
some of us still thought
Vietnam was a suburb of Korea. (10-19)

While Lorde was intensely committed to the Black Arts and African-American liberation movements, she was equally concerned with issues of gender. Throughout her life she was active in both white and black feminist movements. She also had friendships and professional relationships with a number of key women activists and writers over the course of her life, including Toni Cade Bambara, Michelle Cliff, Adrienne Rich, Sonia Sanchez, and Barbara Smith. She was troubled by the strain of Black Nationalist thinking that viewed issues of gender as distractions from the primary issues of race.

At the same time, she was critical of white feminists who viewed issues of race as less important than issues of gender. "When I say I am a Black feminist," she asserts, "I mean I recognize that my power as well as my primary oppressions come as a result of my Blackness as well as my womanness, and therefore my struggles on both these fronts are inseparable" (qtd. in Kulii 462). In the poem "Who Said it Was Simple," Lorde places herself in a coffee house where she is waiting with other women before a demonstration. She notices that the waiter passes by a black customer to serve the white women—who are free to take part in the demonstration because black "girls" are at home taking care of their children. The women are oblivious to the waiter's discrimination against the black customer, as well as to their own privilege. Lorde says of herself:

But I who am bound by my mirror
as well as my bed
see causes in colour
as well as sex

and sit here wondering
which me will survive
all these liberations. (12-18)

Some of Lorde's best known essays, such as "An Open Letter to Mary Daly" and "The Master's Tools Will Never Dismantle the Master's House," directly confront white feminists' racist blindness and refusal to acknowledge their own privilege. In "An Open Letter" she challenges feminist theologian Mary Daly about her study of the nature and function of the Goddess, *Gyn/Ecology: The Metaethics of Radical Feminism* (1978), which, in Lorde's view, simultaneously twisted and erased Black women's histories and mythological heritages: "To dismiss our Black foremothers may well be to dismiss where european women learned to love. As an African-american woman in white patriarchy, I am used to having my archetypal experience distorted and trivialized, but it is terribly painful to feel it being done by a woman whose knowledge so touches my own" (67-8).

In addition to battling sexism in race movements and racism in gender movements, Lorde courageously resisted the homophobia she faced as a lesbian. She believed that people's hostility to homosexuals stemmed from their insecurities about their own identities, and decided that her best "self-protection" would be complete openness about her sexuality. Her first public declaration of her lesbianism took place in the early seventies at a woman-owned bookstore where she read "Love Poem":

Speak earth and bless me with what is richest
make sky flow honey out of my hips
rigid as mountains
spread over a valley
carved out by the mouth of rain.

And I knew when I entered her I was
high wind in her forests hollow

fingers whispering sound
honey flowed
from the split cup
impaled on a lance of tongues
on the tips of her breasts on her navel
and my breath
howling into her entrances
through lungs of pain.

Greedy as herring-gulls
or a child
I swing out over the earth
over and over
again.

When "Love Poem" was later published in *Ms. Magazine*, Lorde posted it on a wall in the English Department of John Jay College of Criminal Justice in Manhattan, where she was teaching courses in race and in writing. In a 1979 interview with Adrienne Rich, Lorde said of her decision to make her lesbianism more widely known in her public and professional lives: "I knew, as I had always known, that the only way you can head people off from using who you are against you is to be honest and open first, to talk about yourself before they talk about you. . . . when you [Rich] heard me read 'Love Poem,' I had already made up my mind that I wasn't going to be worrying any more over who knows and who doesn't know that I have always loved women" (98-9).

Lorde contended that racism, sexism, and homophobia stemmed from the same root: "an inability to recognize the notion of difference as a dynamic human force, one which is enriching rather than threatening to the defined self, when there are shared goals" ("Scratching the Surface" 45). Overwhelmed by the tugging among all the different interest groups with which she worked concerning who is the most oppressed, Lorde sarcastically observes in "Revolution is One Form of Social Change":

> When the man is busy
> making niggers
> it doesn't matter
> much
> what shade
> you are. (1-6)

Lorde struggled bravely for personal authenticity, and wished the same for everyone—her loved ones, her students, and all those who live in oppressive circumstances. "Be who you are and will be," the first line of "For Each of You," the first poem in *From a Land Where Other People Live*, is both her affirmation of and charge to each individual. Thus, from the beginning, her poems embodied hope, love, healing, and a call to engagement. The poem continues:

> learn to cherish
> that boisterous Black Angel that drives you
> up one day and down another
> protecting the place where your power rises
> running like hot blood
> from the same source
> as your pain. (1-8)

Much of Lorde's poetry affirms the web of connections that binds all human beings, a web that extends across time, space, and cultures. We see her strengthening this web in the poems about her children, her mother, and in her references to the valiant men and women of many cultures who were her contemporaries, as well as those of the past. We also see this affirmation of bonds reaching into the past in the poems in which she reclaims the orishas of her African heritage.

For Lorde, it was not sufficient to seek fulfillment in the present; it was also necessary to build the institutions and networks that would sustain community into the future. Lorde's commitment to future generations was especially evident in her teaching and in her efforts to institutionalize African-American Studies. She believed it was essential to pass on to her students the lifelong practice of critical self-examination and critical analysis of the world in which they live. In the poem "Blackstudies" she envisions her students as having learned these lessons, and holding her in their memory:

> The chill wind is beating down from the high places.
> My students wait outside my door
> searching condemning listening
> for what I am sworn to tell them
> for what they least want to hear
> clogging the only exit from the 17th floor
> begging in their garbled language
> beyond judgement or understanding
> "oh speak to us now mother for soon
> we will not need you
> only your memory
> teaching us questions." (142-153)

This aspect of Lorde's work and life is an essential part of the Broadside poets' legacy: individuals committed to doing not only the work they loved but to creating institutions and structures that would outlive them and benefit future generations. My favorite Lorde poem, "The Seventh Sense," states this commitment in the most basic of terms:

> Women
> who build nations
> learn
> to love

men
who build nations
learn
to love
children
building sand castles
by the rising sea.

Audre Lorde died on November 17, 1992 in St. Croix, after a long battle with cancer that she made public through her book, *The Cancer Journals* (1980). Through this battle, too, she taught others how to connect to their own power and each other. Before her death, Lorde took the name "Gamba Adisa," meaning "Warrior, She Who Makes Her Meaning Known" in an African naming ceremony (De Veaux 365). This name confirms all she struggled to be during her life and honors her African cultural heritage. For me, Lorde's most important lessons are that we must name ourselves and resist the injustices we see. We must not be silent in the face of oppression of any kind. For those of you who are embarking on the road to becoming a poet, I leave you with her words: "Poetry is not a luxury."

Works Cited

Bereano, Nancy K. Introduction. *Sister Outsider*. 7-12.

De Veaux, Alexis. *Warrior Poet: A Biography of Audre Lorde*. New York: W. W. Norton & Company, 2004.

Kulii, Beverly Threatt. "Lorde, Audre." *The Oxford Companion to African American Literature*. Eds. William L. Andrews, Frances Smith Foster, and Trudier Harris. NY: Oxford UP, 1997. 461-3.

Lorde, Audre. "Audre Lorde: Interview" with Karla M. Hammond. *Denver Quarterly* Vol. 16, No.1 (Spring 1981): 10-27.

———. *The Cancer Journals*. Argyle, NY: Spinsters Ink, 1980.

———. "An Interview: Audre Lorde and Adrienne Rich." *Sister Outsider*. 81-109.

———. "The Master's Tools Will Never Dismantle the Master's House." *Sister Outsider*. 110-113.

———. "An Open Letter to Mary Daly." *Sister Outsider*. 66-71.

———. "Poetry Is Not a Luxury." *Sister Outsider*. 36-39.

———. "Scratching the Surface: Some Notes on Barriers to Women and Loving." *Sister Outsider*. 45-52.

———. *Sister Outsider: Essays and Speeches by Audre Lorde*. The Crossing Press Feminist Series. Trumansburg, NY: The Crossing Press, 1984.

For Each of You

Be who you are and will be
learn to cherish
that boisterous Black Angel that drives you
up one day and down another
protecting the place where your power rises
running like hot blood
from the same source
as your pain.

When you are hungry
learn to eat
whatever sustains you
until morning
but do not be misled by details
simply because you live them.

Do not let your head deny
your hands
any memory of what passes through them
nor your eyes
nor your heart
everything can be used
except what is wasteful
(you will need
to remember this when you are accused of destruction.)

Even when they are dangerous
examine the heart of those machines you hate
before you discard them
and never mourn the lack of their power
lest you be condemned
to relive them.
If you do not learn to hate
you will never be lonely
enough
to love easily
nor will you always be brave
although it does not grow any easier
Do not pretend to convenient beliefs
even when they are righteous
you will never be able to defend your city
while shouting.

Remember our sun
is not the most noteworthy star
only the nearest.

Respect whatever pain you bring back
from your dreaming
but do not look for new gods
in the sea
nor in any part of a rainbow
Each time you love

love as deeply
as if it were
forever
only nothing is
eternal.

Speak proudly to your children
where ever you may find them
tell them
you are the offspring of slaves
and your mother was
a princess
in darkness.

Equinox

My daughter marks the day that spring begins.
I cannot celebrate spring without remembering
how the bodies of unborn children
bake in their mothers flesh like ovens
consecrated to the flame that eats them
lit by mobiloil and easternstandard
Unborn children in their blasted mothers
floating like small monuments
in an ocean of oil.

The year my daughter was born
DuBois died in Accra while I
marched into Washington
to a death knell of dreaming
which 250,000 others mistook for a hope
believing only Birmingham's black children
were being pounded into mortar in churches
that year
some of us still thought
Vietnam was a suburb of Korea.

Then John Kennedy fell off the roof
of Southeast Asia
and shortly afterward my whole house burned down
with nobody in it
and on the following sunday my borrowed radio announced
that Malcolm was shot dead
and I ran to reread
all that he had written
because death was becoming such an excellent measure
of prophecy
As I read his words the dark mangled children
came streaming out of the atlas
Hanoi Angola Guinea-Bissau Mozambique Pnam-Phen
merged into Bedford-Stuyvesant and Hazelhurst Mississippi
haunting my New York tenement that terribly bright summer
while Detroit and Watts and San Francisco were burning

I lay awake in stifling Broadway nights afraid
for whoever was growing in my belly
and suppose it started earlier than planned
who would I trust to take care that my daughter
did not eat poisoned roaches
when I was gone?

If she did, it doesn't matter
because I never knew it.
Today both children came home from school
talking about spring and peace
and I wonder if they will ever know it
I want to tell them we have no right to spring
because our sisters and brothers are burning
because every year the oil grows thicker
and even the earth is crying
because black is beautiful but currently
going out of style
that we must be very strong
and love each other
in order to go on living.

Black Mother Woman

I cannot recall you gentle
yet through your heavy love
I have become
an image of your once delicate flesh
split with deceitful longings.

When strangers come and compliment me
your aged spirit takes a bow
jingling with pride
but once you hid that secret
in the center of furies
hanging me
with deep breasts and wiry hair
with your own split flesh
and long suffering eyes
buried in myths of little worth.

But I have peeled away your anger
down to the core of love
and look mother
I Am
a dark temple where your true spirit rises
beautiful
and tough as chestnut

stanchion against your nightmare of weakness
and if my eyes conceal
a squadron of conflicting rebellions
I learned from you
to define myself
through your denials.

The Seventh Sense

Women
who build nations
learn
to love
men
who build nations
learn
to love
children
building sand castles
by the rising sea.

Teacher

I make my children promises in wintry afternoons
like lunchtime stories
when my feet hurt from talking too much
and not enough movement except in my own
worn down at the heel shoes
except in the little circle of broken down light
I am trapped in
the intensities of my own (our) situation
where what we need and do not have
deadens us
and promises sound like destruction
white snowflakes clog the passages
drifting through the halls and corridors
while I tell stories with no ending
at lunchtime
the children's faces bear uneasy smiles
like a heavy question
I provide food with a frightening efficiency
the talk is free/dom meaning state
condition of being
We are elementary forces colliding in free fall.

And who will say I made promises
better kept in confusion
than time

grown tall and straight in a season of snow
in a harsh time of the sun that withers
who will say as they build
ice castles at noon
living the promises I made
these children
who will say
look—we have laid out the new cities
with more love than our dreams
Who will hear
freedom's bell deaden
in the clang of the gates of the prisons
where snow-men melt into darkness
unforgiven and so remembered
while the hot noon speaks in a fiery voice?

How we romped through so many winters
made snowballs play at war
rubbing snow against our brown faces
and they tingled and grew bright
in the winter sun
instead of chocolate we rolled snow
over our tongues
until it melted like sugar
burning the cracks in our lips
and we shook our numbed fingers
all the way home

remembering
summer was coming.

As the promises I make children
sprout like wheat from early spring's wager
who will hear freedom
ring in the chains of promise
who will forget the curse
of the outsider
who will not recognize our season
as free
who will say
Promise corrupts
what it does not invent.

Moving Out or
The End of Cooperative Living

I am so glad to be moving
away from this prison for black and white faces
assaulting each other with our joint oppression
competing for who pays the highest price for this privilege
I am so glad I am moving
technicoloured complaints aimed at my head
mash themselves on my door like mosquitoes
sweep like empty ladles through the lobby of my eyes
each time my lips move sideways
the smile shatters
on the in thing that races
dictator through our hallways
on concrete faces on soul compactors
on the rhetoric of incinerators and plastic drapes
for the boiler room
on legends of broken elevators
blowing my morning cool
avoiding me in the corridors
dropping their load on my face down 24 stories
of lives in a spectrumed madhouse
pavilion of gnats and nightmare remembering
once we all saved like beggars
to buy our way into this castle
of fantasy and forever now
I am so glad to be moving.

Last month a tenant was asked to leave
because someone saw him
wandering one morning up and down the tenth floor
with no clothes on
having locked himself out the night before
with the garbage
he could not fit into the incinerator
but it made no difference
the floor captain cut the leads to his cable TV
and he left covered in tangled wires of shame
his apartment was reconsecrated by a fumigator
I am so glad I am moving

Although workmen will descend at $100 an hour
to scrape my breath from the walls
to refinish the air and the floors with their eyes
and charge me with the exact amount
of whatever I have coming back to me
called equity
I am so glad to be moving
from the noise of psychic footsteps
beating a tune that is not my own
louder than any other sound in the neighborhood
except the blasting that goes on all day and all night
from the city's new toilet being built
outside the main entrance
from the spirits who live in the locks

of the other seven doors
bellowing secrets of living hells revealed
but not shared
for everybody's midnights know what the walls hide
our toilets are made of glass
wired for sound

24 stories
full of tears flushing at midnight
our only community room
children set their clocks to listen at the tissue walls
gazing upward from their stools
from one flight to another
catching the neighbors in private struggles
next morning it will all be discussed
at length in the elevators
with no secrets left
I am so glad to be moving
no more coming home at night to dream
of caged puppies
grinding their teeth into cartoonlike faces
that half plead and half snicker
then fold under and vanish
back into snarling strangers
I am so glad I am moving.

But when this grim house goes
slipping into the sewer prepared for it
then this whole city can read
its own obituary
written on the broken record of dreams
of ordinary people
who wanted what they could not get
and so pretended to be someone else
ordinary people having
what they never learned to want
themselves
and so becoming
pretension concretized.

Generation II

A Black girl
going
into the woman
her mother
desired
and prayed for
walks alone
and afraid
of both
their angers.

Conclusion

Passing men in the street who are dead
becomes a common occurrence
but loving one of them
is no solution.
I believe in love as I believe in our children
but I was born Black and without illusions
and my vision
which differs from yours
is clear
although sometimes restricted.

I have watched you at midnight
moving through casual sleep
wishing I could afford the non-desperate dreams
that stir you
to wither and fade into partial solutions.
Your nights are wintery long and very young
full of symbols of purity and forgiveness
and a meek jesus that rides through your cities
on a barren ass whose braying
does not include a future tense.
But I wear my nights as I wear my life
and my dying
absolute and unforgiven
nuggets of compromise and decision

fossilized by fierce midsummer sun
and when I dream
I move through a Black land
where the future
glows eternal and green
but where the symbols for now
are bloody and unrelenting
rooms
where confused children
with wooden stumps for fingers
play at war
who cannot pick up their marbles
and run away home
whenever nightmare threatens.

The Winds of Orisha

I

This land will not always be foreign.
How many of its women ache to bear their stories
robust and screaming like the earth erupting grain
or thrash in padded chains mute as bottles
hands fluttering traces of resistance
on the backs of once lovers
half the truth
knocking in the brain like an angry steampipe

how many
long to work or split open
so bodies venting into silence
can plan the next move?

Tiresias took 500 years they say to progress into woman
growing smaller and darker and more powerful
until nut-like, she went to sleep in a bottle
Tiresias took 500 years to grow into woman
so do not despair of your sons.

      II
Impatient legends speak through my flesh
changing this earths formation
spreading
I will become myself
an incantation
dark raucous many-shaped characters
leaping back and forth across bland pages
and Mother Yemonja raises her breasts to begin my labour
near water
the beautiful Oshun and I lie down together
in the heat of her body truth my voice comes stronger
Shango will be my brother roaring out of the sea
earth shakes our darkness swelling into each other
warning winds will announce us living
as Oya, Oya my sister my daughter
destroys the crust of the tidy beaches
and Eshu's black laughter turns up the neat sleeping sand.

III

The heart of this country's tradition is its wheat men
dying for money
dying for water for markets for power
over all people's children
they sit in their chains on their dry earth
before nightfall
telling tales as they wait for their time
of completion
hoping the young ones can hear them
earth-shaking fears wreath their blank weary faces
most of them have spent their lives and their wives
in labour
most of them have never seen beaches
but as Oya my sister moves out of the mouths
of their sons and daughters against them
I will swell up from the pages of their daily heralds
leaping out of the almanacs
instead of an answer to their search for rain
    they will read me
the dark cloud
meaning something entire
and different.

When the winds of Orisha blow
even the roots of grass
quicken.

Who Said It Was Simple

There are so many roots to the tree of anger
that sometimes the branches shatter
before they bear.

Sitting in Nedicks
the women rally before they march
discussing the problematic girls
they hire to make them free.
An almost white counterman passes
a waiting brother to serve them first
and the ladies neither notice nor reject
the slighter pleasures of their slavery.
But I who am bound by my mirror
as well as my bed
see causes in colour
as well as sex

and sit here wondering
which me will survive
all these liberations.

To My Daughter The Junkie On A Train

Children we have not borne
bedevil us by becoming
themselves
painfully sharp and unavoidable
like a needle in our flesh.

Coming home on the subway from a PTA meeting
of minds committed like murder
or suicide
to their own private struggle
a long-legged girl with a horse in her brain
slumps down beside me
begging to be ridden asleep
for the price of a midnight train
free from desire.
Little girl on the nod
if we are measured by the dreams we avoid
then you are the nightmare
of all sleeping mothers
rocking back and forth
the dead weight of your arms
locked about our necks
heavier than our habit
of looking for reasons.

My corrupt concern will not replace
what you once needed
but I am locked into my own addictions
and offer you my help, one eye
out
for my own station.
Roused and deprived
your costly dream explodes
into a terrible technicoloured laughter
at my failure
up and down across the aisle
women avert their eyes
as the other mothers who became useless
curse their children who became junk.

Now

Woman power
is
Black power
is
Human power
is
always feeling
my heart beats
as my eyes open
as my hands move
as my mouth speaks

I am
are you

Ready.

Love Poem

Speak earth and bless me with what is richest
make sky flow honey out of my hips
rigid as mountains
spread over a valley
carved out by the mouth of rain.

And I knew when I entered her I was
high wind in her forests hollow
fingers whispering sound
honey flowed
from the split cup
impaled on a lance of tongues
on the tips of her breasts on her navel
and my breath
howling into her entrances
through lungs of pain.

Greedy as herring-gulls
or a child
I swing out over the earth
over and over
again.

Separation

The stars dwindle
and will not reward me
even in triumph.

It is possible
to shoot a man
in self defense
and still notice
how his red blood
decorates the snow.

Even

Nothing
is sorry
sameness
a trap called
no dream remembered.

There are no iron creases
in the mind's coat
no past season's shelter
against tonight's rain

every stain
the same
sin of unlonging
lying
pouring
like windless brown rags
of summer falling
away from the trees.

Revolution Is One Form Of Social Change

When the man is busy
making niggers
it doesn't matter
much
what shade
you are.

If he runs out of one
particular color
he can always switch
to size
and when he's finished
off the big ones
he'll just change

to sex
which is
after all
where it all began.

All Hallows Eve

My mother taught each one of us
to pray
as soon as we could talk
and every Halloween
to comfort us
before she went to work
my mother cooked fresh pumpkin with brown sugar
and placing penny candles in our windows
she said her yearly prayers
for all our dead.

As soon as mother left us
we feasted on warm pumpkin
until the empty pot sang out its earthy smell
and then, our mouths free,
we told each other stories of other Halloweens
making our wishes true
while from our windows
we watched the streets grow dark
and the witches slowly gathering below.

In each window
a penny candle in its own dish of water
flickered around our tales
throughout the evening.
Most of them burnt down
before our stories ended
and we went to bed
without replacing them.

Viet-Nam Addenda
for/Clifford

Genocide doesn't only mean bombs
at high noon and the cameras
panning in on the ruptured stomach
of somebody else's pubescent daughter.
A small difference in time and space
names that war
while we live
117th street at high noon
powerlessly familiar.
We are raped of our children
in silence
giving birth to spots quickly
rubbed out at dawn
on the streets of Jamaica

or left
all the time in the world
for the nightmare of idleness
to turn their hands
against us.

Sacrifice

The only hungers left
are the hungers allowed us.

By the light of our sacred street lamps
by whatever maps we are sworn to follow
pleasure will betray us
unless we do what we must do
without
wanting to do it
feel the enemy stone give way in retreat
without pleasure or satisfaction
we look the other way
as our dreams come true
as our bloody hands move over history
writing
we have come
we have done
what we came to do.

Pulling down statues of rock from their high places
we must level the expectation
upon which they stand
waiting for us
to fulfill their image
waiting
for our feet to replace them.

Unless we refuse to sleep
even one night in houses of marble
the sight of our children's false pleasure
will undo us
for our children have grown
in the shadow of what was
the shape of marble
between their eyes and the sun
but we do not wish to stand
like great marble statues
between our children's eyes
and their sun.

Learning all
we can use
only what is vital
The only sacrifice of worth
is the sacrifice of desire.

Blackstudies

I

A chill wind sweeps the high places.
On the ground I watch bearers of wood
carved in the image of old and mistaken gods
labour in search of weapons against the blind dancers
who balance great dolls on their shoulders
as they scramble over the same earth
searching for food.

In a room on the 17th floor my spirit is choosing
I am afraid of speaking
the truth
in a room on the 17th floor
my body is dreaming
it sits
bottom pinned to a table
eating perpetual watermelon inside my own head
while young girls assault my door
with curse rags
stiff with their mothers old secrets
covering up their new promise
with old desires no longer their need
with old satisfactions they never enjoyed
outside my door they are waiting
with questions that feel like judgments
when they are unanswered.

The palms of my hands have black marks running across them
So are signed makers of myth
who are sworn through our blood to give
legend
children will come to understand
to speak out living words like this poem
that knits truth into fable
to leave my story behind
though I fall through cold wind condemned
to nursing old gods for a new heart
debtless and without colour
while my flesh is covered by mouths
whose noise keeps my real wants secret.

I do not want to lie. I have loved other
tall young women deep into their colour
who now crawl over a bleached earth
bent into questionmarks
ending a sentence of men
who pretended to be brave.
Even this
can be an idle defense
protecting the lies I am trying to reject.

I am afraid
that the mouths I feed will turn against me
will refuse to swallow in the silence
I am warning them to avoid
I am afraid
they will kernel me out like a walnut
extracting the nourishing seed
as my husk stains their lips
with the mixed colours of my pain.

While I sit choosing the voice
in which my children hear my prayers
above the wind
they will follow the black roads out of my hands
unencumbered by the weight of my remembered sorrows
by the weight of my remembered sorrows
they will use my legends to shape their own language
and make it ruler
measuring the distance between my hungers
and their own purpose.
I am afraid
They will discard my most ancient nightmares
where the fallen gods became demon
instead of dust.

II

Just before light devils woke me
trampling my flesh into fruit
that would burst in the sun
until I came to despise every evening
fearing a strange god at the fall of each night
and when my mother punished me
by sending me to bed without my prayers
I had no names for darkness.

I do not know whose words protected me
whose tales or tears prepared me
for this trial on the 17th floor
I do not know whose legends blew
through my mothers furies
but somehow they fell through my sleeping lips
like the juice of forbidden melons
and the little black seeds were sown
throughout my heart
like closed and waiting eyes
and although demons rode me
until I rose up a child of morning
deep roads sprouted over the palms
of my hidden fists
dark and growing.

III

Chill winds swirl around these high blank places.
It is the time when the bearer of hard news
is destroyed for the message
when it is heard.
A. B. is a poet who says our people
fear our own beauty
has not made us hard enough
to survive victory
but he too has written his children upon women
I hope with love.
I bear mine alone in the mouth of the enemy
upon a desk on the 17th floor
swept bare by cold winds
bright as neon.

IV

Their demon father rode me just before daylight
I learned his tongue as he reached
for my hands at dawn
before he could touch the palms of my hands
to devour my children
I learned his language
I ate him
and left his bones mute in the noon sun.

Now all the words in my legend come garbled
except anguish.
Visions of chitterlings I never ate
strangle me in a nightmare of leaders
at crowded meetings to study our problems
I move awkward and ladylike
through four centuries of unused bathtubs
that never smile
not even an apologetic grin
I worry on nationalist holidays
make a fetish of lateness
with limp unbelieved excuses
shunning the use of pronouns
as an indirect assult
what skin I have left
unbetrayed by scouring
uncovered by mouths that shriek
but do not speak my real wants
glistens and twinkles blinding all beholders
"But I just washed them, Mommy!"

Only the black marks on my hands itch and flutter
shredding my words and wherever they fall
the earth springs up denials
that I pay for
only the dark roads over my palms
wait for my voice
to follow.

V

The chill wind is beating down from the high places.
My students wait outside my door
searching condemning listening
for what I am sworn to tell them
for what they least want to hear
clogging the only exit from the 17th floor
begging in their garbled language
beyond judgement or understanding
"oh speak to us now mother for soon
we will not need you
only your memory
teaching us questions."

Stepping into my self
I open the door
and leap groundward
wondering
what shall they carve for weapons
what shall they grow for food.

Sources

Lorde, Audre. *From a Land Where Other People Live*. Detroit: Broadside Press, 1973.

For Each of You
Equinox
Black Mother Woman
The Seventh Sense
Teacher
Moving Out or The End of Cooperative Living
Generation II
Conclusion
The Winds of Orisha
Who Said It Was Simple

Lorde, Audre. *New York Head Shop and Museum*. Detroit: Broadside Press, 1974.

To My Daughter The Junkie On A Train
Now
Love Poem
Separation
Even
Revolution Is One Form Of Social Change
All Hallows Eve
Viet-Nam Addenda
Sacrifice
Blackstudies

Lynda Koolish © 2004

haki madhubuti

Haki Madhubuti: A Voice of Our Own
Sondai K. Lester

Haki Madhubuti was one of the most powerful and insightful voices to come out of Broadside Press.[1] Along with the other young black poets of that era, Madhubuti dramatically altered the structure and language of black poetry. Their poetry was revolutionary, not only in its content, which called for the building of a Black Nation and not the dream of integration, but also in how they delivered that much-needed message. Madhubuti was raised in the blue collar, highly politicized cities of Detroit and Chicago. He spent countless hours tuned in to John Coltrane's *Love Supreme*, *Expressions*, and *Alabama*, and writing poetry that broke the accepted rules of literary expression. Madhubuti, through his Broadside Press publications, created a revolutionary literature that would compel his contemporary readers to think in a completely different way about themselves and the world.

The poetry of Haki Madhubuti was straight from the streets. It expressed, in language and symbols familiar to the masses of black people trapped in the dismal conditions of oppressed exploited urban ghettoes, the dynamics and contradictions of black life. His poetry completely eroded the lies, subterfuge, façades, and pretenses that helped to conceal the reality of black life. He made it clear that the well-dressed, college-educated, materially-affluent black executive was just as oppressed as the black man toiling and sweating in the hot dusty steel mills of Pennsylvania. Madhubuti's poems reached down into the very soul of black people and rocked our world. He exposed the inconsistencies of black life—from the pseudo-black revolutionary talking black and sleeping white to the slick-talking pimp exploiting and degrading black women while claiming to love his black mother.

Madhubuti took the word "nigger" and turned it from a racial epithet into a symbol of the slave mentality with its subsequent self-destructive pattern of behaviors that helps to perpetuate black oppression. A "nigger" is the pathological product of a prolonged experience of oppression and powerlessness, one of the external tangible circumstances of human life that are products of the intangible inner realities of those who share a social reality. Madhubuti believed that social systems emerge and are sustained by a set of ideas accepted as logical and legitimate by the vast majority of people living within those systems. In a social system made up of oppressor and oppressed, both unwittingly conspire together to maintain that world of inequity and injustice. This happens without conscious awareness on the part of either group; it happens because both have been socially conditioned to believe in the myth of the inherent biological superiority of the oppressor. Thus, for Madhubuti, the moral appeal for black non-violent resistance as a vehicle to realize the dream of equal integration into the oppressor's world that characterized early civil rights movements in the US was based on a misunderstanding of the nature of power and the function of social systems.

The oppressor, as the primary recipient of all the material and psychological advantages of the world of oppressor and oppressed, has no compelling reason to voluntarily think, feel, or act differently. As such, the onus of responsibility for transforming that world falls upon the oppressed. Madhubuti states clearly in his writings that if we are to escape from our dismal world of racial oppression, we must first change—change our minds and cease to be "niggers"—before our external world of racial oppression and powerlessness can be changed. As I see it, the poem "A Poem to Complement other Poems," from the classic collection of his writings, *Don't Cry, Scream* (1969*)*, most completely and vividly captures Madhubuti's perception of the nature of the black struggle for independence and power. Hear his words:

> . . . change. now now change. for
> the better change.
> read a change. live a change. read a blackpoem.
> change. be the realpeople.
> change. blackpoems
> will change:
> . . . .
>
> change change your change change change.
> your
> mind nigger. (59-64, 75-77)

In a world where black people seemed to have no voice of their own, Madhubuti became our voice. He said what we needed to say, what we wanted to say in a voice and language we could understand. In his voice and words we felt within us the power of the humanity our oppressor sought to deny.

In a very intimate way, Madhubuti's words spoke most directly to the inner contradictions and confusion plaguing black men. From the earliest days of chattel slavery until now, black men have been plagued and stifled by irreconcilable conflicting identities. On one hand, there is the God-given identity of all men, equal in intelligence and potential to function in the world; then, there is the oppressor's socially imposed identity of a black man—with intelligence and potential inferior to any white man. Liberated man versus permanently enslaved man. Man who could protect his family and defend his people versus man helpless to protect or defend anyone. Madhubuti was the voice of the liberated black male proudly and defiantly asserting his humanity as a black man.

Haki Madhubuti gave voice to a part of me that I vaguely knew existed but, for the life of me, could not express. As a young black man my life was burdened each day by a pathological inner conflict constantly threatening to tear me apart. I saw the battered face of Emmett Till on the cover of *Jet* magazine and felt something deep and powerful inside, but I did not know what it was or how to express it. I watched the savagery faced by black students not much older than me at Central High School in Little Rock and felt something mysterious within, but had no voice to express it. I saw the water hoses almost cut young black kids in half, and I watched as hateful racist policemen urged vicious dogs to attack them in Birmingham. Like a rising storm, I felt I should do or say something, but I had no voice to express it. And then, in 1965, before I was mentally overcome by my inner turmoil, along came Broadside Press and the writings of Haki Madhubuti, giving me a vehicle to discover my own voice and to defiantly assert my own humanity.

Broadside Press and the cadre of young radical black writers it nurtured and published like Haki Madhubuti transformed the consciousness of a people. Between 1966 and 1976 the poetry of Haki Madhubuti was read, discussed, and performed by black people on college campuses, in inner-city public schools, penitentiaries, and neighborhood community centers all across this country. Black people, inspired by the impassioned hope and expectation for change growing out of the Civil Rights movement and the call for Black Power, searched feverishly for words to give that hope a meaningful perspective. Words to define an identity compatible with that hope and expectation. Words to bring the nature of their struggle into focus. They found those sacred words in Madhubuti's *Think Black* (1966), *Black Pride* (1968), *Don't Cry, Scream* (1969), *We Walk the Way of the New World* (1970), *Book of Life* (1973), and *From Plan to Planet* (1973), all of which were published by Broadside Press. Not since the fiery oratory and controversial writings of the Honorable Marcus Mosiah Garvey forty-five years prior had they heard their own language, the language of the streets, so powerfully used to articulate their desires and experiences, or to motivate them to identify so personally with the struggle to liberate black people.

Like so many young people coming of age during the idealism and resistance to the status quo of the Civil Rights movement, Madhubuti came under influences that led to his conversion and mental liberation from the ideas and world of his oppressor. These influences led to an evolution in his consciousness. He recounts in an interview with Angela Ards in *Black Issues Book Review*, March-April 2002, that reading Richard Wright was "the first time I had been smacked in the face with the *power of ideas*" (emphasis added, 44). He went on to absorb the writings of Chester Himes, Gwendolyn Brooks, Margaret Walker, and other renowned African American writers, saying that these writers served as anchors "for boys and girls like me who were looking for *something in our language* to hold onto and build hopes and dreams on" (emphasis added, 44). Madhubuti's own mental liberation occurred as a result of drawing upon the assembled legacy of writings by black authors who had already broken free mentally and discovered their own independent black voices.

At some point in the journey on this earth, each generation must discover its own voice and language in order to give expression to its own humanity and to its particular perspective on the struggle to discover the divine purpose and meaning of their existence. Broadside Press became the channel for the generation of black Americans coming of age in the sixties and seventies to give voice to the experience of their humanity. Dudley Randall inscribed on broadsides and distributed a voice that the major publishing houses at that time defined as "non-intellectual" and even "treasonous" in its content. Broadside provided the critical institutional context necessary for the distribution of ideas that could build a black counter-culture based upon a rejection of the oppressor's myth of black inferiority, and a creative outlet for those struggling to think independently of their oppressor. Those who came to understand the power of ideas became potent agents of change. As a Broadside author, Madhubuti was able to contribute to the on-going evolving text of liberating ideas—ideas that dramatically changed and continue to change black people and lead to their participation in struggles that can bring about a radical transformation of their world. Haki Madhubuti, in gaining his own voice through Broadside Press, helped me and countless other young black men and women through his writings to experience our humanity and discover our own voices in our own language. Indeed, Haki Madhubuti continues to provide new generations of black youth with a voice and language to build their own hopes and dreams. Through his own Third World Press, which in 2001 celebrated its thirty-fifth anniversary, he has continued to publish poetry and essays on the reality of life for the masses of black people across the world. Across four decades he has been an inspiration and source of enlightenment for his people, and for this we will be forever grateful.

Works Cited

Asanti, Ta'Shia. "Celebrating the Brothers: The Awesome Work of Haki Madhubuti." *Urban Spectrum on the Web* 15.11 (Feb. 2002): 21 pars. 13 June 2002 <http://www.urbanspectrum.net/archives/02-Feb/fea.Madhubutimadh.htm>.

Madhubuti, Haki R. "Haki Madhubuti: The Measure of a Man." By Angela Ards. *Black Issues Book Review* 4.2 (March-April 2002): 42-46.

Endnotes

[1] Before 1973, Haki Madhubuti went by the name "Don L. Lee." After a trip to Africa, he was inspired to take a traditional African name. As Ta'Shia Asanti explains in "Celebrating the Brothers: The Awesome Work of Haki Madhubuti," Lee felt that "Haki," meaning "just" or "justice," and "Madhubuti," meaning "accurate" or "dependable," "better encompassed the life he was striving to live and create for his fellows" (par. 9).

THE NEW INTEGRATIONIST

I

seek

integration

of

negroes

with

black

people.

"STEREO"

I can clear a beach or swimming pool without

touching water.

I can make a lunch counter become deserted

in less than an hour.

I can make property value drop by being seen

in a realtor's tower.

I ALONE can make the word of God have little

or no meaning to many

in Sunday morning's prayer hour.

I have Power,

BLACK POWER.

RE-ACT FOR ACTION
(for brother H. Rap Brown)

re-act to animals:
                    cage them in zoos.
re-act to inhumanism:
                        make them human.
re-act to nigger toms:
                            with spiritual acts of love & forgiveness
                            or with real acts of force.
re-act to yr/self:
                    or are u too busy tryen to be cool
                    like tony curtis & twiggy?
re-act to whi-te actors:
                        understand their actions;
                        faggot actions & actions against yr/dreams
re-act to yr/brothers & sisters:
                                love.
re-act to whi-te actions:
                        with real acts of blk/action.
                        BAM BAM BAM

re-act to act against actors
who act out pig-actions against
your acts & actions   that keep
you re-acting against their act & actions
stop.
act in a way that will cause them
to act the way you want them to act

in accordance with yr/acts & actions:
                                        human acts for human beings
re-act
NOW niggers
& you won't have to
act
false-actions
at
your/children's graves.

FIRST IMPRESSIONS ON A POET'S DEATH
                              (for Conrad Kent Rivers)

blk/poets die

from

not being

read

& from, maybe,

too-much

leg.

some drank

themselves

into

non-poets,

but most

poets who poet
seldom

die
from

overexposure.

Gwendolyn Brooks

she doesn't wear
costume jewelry
& she knew that walt disney
was/is making a fortune off
false-eyelashes and that time magazine is the
authority on the knee/grow.
her makeup is total-real.

a negro english instructor called her:
    "a fine negro poet."
a whi-te critic said:
    "she's a credit to the negro race."
somebody else called her:
    "a pure negro writer."
johnnie mae, who's a senior in high school said:
    "she & langston are the only negro poets we've
    read in school and i understand her."
pee wee used to carry one of her poems around in his back pocket;
    the one about being cool. that was befo pee wee
    was cooled by a cop's warning shot.

into the sixties
a word was born . . . . BLACK
& with black came poets
& from the poet's ball points came:

black doubleblack purpleblack blueblack beenblack was
black daybeforeyesterday blackerthan ultrablack super
black blackblack yellowblack niggerblack blackwhi-te-
      man
blackerthanyoueverbes ¼ black unblack coldblack clear
black my momma's blackerthanyourmomma pimpleblack
      fall
black so black we can't even see you black on black in
black by black technically black mantanblack winter
black coolblack 360degreesblack coalblack midnight
black black when it's convenient rustyblack moonblack
black starblack summerblack electronblack spaceman
black shoeshineblack jimshoeblack underwearblack ugly
black auntjimammablack, uncleben'srice black
      williebest
black blackisbeautifulblack i justdiscoveredblack negro
black unsubstanceblack.

and everywhere the
lady "negro poet"
appeared the poets were there.
they listened & questioned
& went home feeling uncomfortable/unsound & so-
      untogether
they read/re-read/wrote & re-wrote
& came back the next time to tell the
lady "negro poet"
how beautiful she was/is & how she had helped them
& she came back with:

how necessary they were and how they've helped her.
the poets walked & as space filled the vacuum between
    them & the
lady "negro poet"
u could hear one of the blackpoets say:
    "bro, they been callin that sister by the wrong name."

But He Was Cool or: he even stopped for green lights

super-cool
ultrablack
a tan/purple
had a beautiful shade.

he had a double-natural
that wd put the sisters to shame.
his dashikis were tailor made
& his beads were imported sea shells
    (from some blk/country i never heard of)
he was triple-hip.

his tikis were hand carved
out of ivory
& came express from the motherland.
he would greet u in swahili
& say good-by in yoruba.

woooooooooooooo-jim he bes so cool & ill tel li gent
      cool-cool is so cool he was un-cooled by
        other niggers' cool
      cool-cool ultracool was bop-cool/ice box
        cool so cool cold cool
      his wine didn't have to be cooled, him was
        air conditioned cool
      cool-cool/real cool made me cool—now
        ain't that cool
      cool-cool so cool him nick-named refrig-
        erator.

cool-cool so cool
he didn't know,
after detroit, newark, chicago &c.,
we had to hip
     cool-cool/ super-cool/ real cool
  that
to be black
is
to be
very-hot.

DON'T CRY, SCREAM

(John Coltrane/from a black poet/
in a basement apt. crying dry tears
of "you ain't gone.")

into the sixties
a trane
came/ out of the
fifties with a
golden boxcar
riding the rails
of novation.
       blowing
       a-melodics
       screeching,
       screaming,
       blasting—
              driving some away,
              (those paper readers who thought
              manhood was something innate)

              bring others in,
              (the few who didn't believe that the
              world existed around established whi
              teness & leonard bernstein)

music that ached.
murdered our minds (we reborn)
born into a neoteric aberration.
& suddenly
you envy the
BLIND man—
you know that he will
hear what you'll never
see.

        your music is like
        my head—nappy black/
        a good nasty feel with
        tangled songs of:
            we-eeeeeeeeee   sing
            WE-EEEeeeeeeeee   loud &
            WE-EEEEEEEEEEEEEEEEE high
                                         with
                                         feeling

a people playing
the sound of me when
i combed it. combed at
it.

i cried for billie holiday.
the blues. we ain't blue
the blues exhibited illusions of manhood.
destroyed by you. Ascension into:

scream-eeeeeeeeeeeeeee-ing   sing
SCREAM-EEEeeeeeeeeeee-ing   loud &
SCREAM-EEEEEEEEEEEEEEE-ing   long with
                                                  feeling

we ain't blue, we are black.
we ain't blue, we are black.
                  (all the blues did was
                  make me cry)
soultrane gone on a trip
he left man images
he was a life-style of
man-makers & annihilator
of attache case carriers.

Trane done went.
(got his hat & left me one)
naw brother,
i didn't cry,
i just—
     Scream-eeeeeeeeeeeeeee-ed   sing loud
     SCREAM-EEEEEEEEEEEEEEEEEEE-ED   & high with
         we-eeeeeeeeeeeeeeeeeeeeee ee   feeling
         WE-EEEEEEeeeeeeeeeEEEEEEEE   letting
         WE-EEEEEEEEEEEEEEEEEEEEEEEE   yr/voice
         WHERE YOU DONE GONE, BROTHER?   break

it hurts, grown babies
dying. born. done caught me
a trane. steel wheels broken
by popsicle sticks. i went out
& tried to buy a nickle bag
with my standard oil card.

        (swung on a faggot who politely
        scratched his ass in my presence.
        he smiled broken teeth stained from
        his over-used tongue. fisted-face.
        teeth dropped in tune with ray
        charles singing "yesterday.")

blonds had more fun—
with snagga-tooth niggers
who saved pennies & pop bottles for week-ends
to play negro & other filthy inventions.
be-bop-en to james brown's
cold sweat—these niggers didn't sweat,
they perspired. & the blond's dye came out,
i ran. she did too, with his pennies, pop bottles
& his mind. tune in next week same time same station
for anti-self in one lesson.

to the negro cow-sissies
who did tchaikovsky &
the beatles & live in
split-level homes & had

split level minds & babies.
who committed the act of
love with their clothes on.
     (who hid in the bathroom to read
     jet mag., who didn't read the chicago
     defender because of the misspelled
     words & had shelves of books by
     europeans on display. untouched. who
     hid their little richard & lightnin'
     slim records & asked: "John who?"

     instant hate.)
they didn't know any better,
brother, they were too busy getting
into debt, expressing humanity &
taking off color.

   SCREAMMMM/we-eeeee/screech/teee improvise
   aheeeeeeeee/screeeeeee/theeee/ee   with
   ahHHHHHHHHH/WEEEEEEEE/scrEEE feeling
    EEEE
   we-eeeeeeWE-EEEEEEEEEWE-EE-EEEEE
the ofays heard you &
were wiped out. spaced.
one clown asked me during,
my favorite things, if
you were practicing.
i fired on the muthafucka & said,
"i'm practicing."

naw brother,
i didn't cry.
i got high off my thoughts—
they kept coming back,
back to destroy me.

& that BLIND man
i don't envy him anymore
i can see his hear
& hear his heard through my pores.
i can see my me. it was truth you gave,
like a daily shit
it had to come.

        can you scream—brother?   very
        can you scream—brother?   soft

i hear you.
i hear you.

and the Gods will too.

Malcolm Spoke/ who listened?
(this poem is for my consciousness too)

he didn't say
wear yr/blackness in
outer garments
& blk/slogans fr/the top 10.

he was fr a long
line of super-cools,
       doo-rag lovers &
       revolutionary pimps.
u are playing that
high-yellow game in blackface
minus the straight hair.
now
it's nappy-black
& air conditioned volkswagens
with undercover whi
te girls who studied faulkner at
smith
& are authorities on "militant"
knee/grows
selling u at jew town rates:
       niggers with wornout tongues
        three for a quarter/or will consider a trade

the double-breasted hipster
has been replaced with a
dashiki wearing rip-off
who went to city college
majoring in physical education.

animals come in all colors.
dark meat will roast as fast as whi-te meat
especially in
the unitedstatesofamerica's
new
self-cleaning ovens.

if we don't listen.

a poem to complement other poems

change.
life if u were a match i wd light u into something beauti-
    ful. change.
change.
for the better into a realreal together thing. change, from
    a make believe
nothing on corn meal and water. change.
change. from the last drop to the first, maxwellhouse
    did. change.

change was a programmer for IBM, thought him was a
    brown computor. change.
colored is something written on southern out-
    houses. change.
greyhound did, i mean they got rest rooms on buses.
    change.
change
change nigger.
saw a nigger hippy, him wanted to be different. changed.
saw a nigger liberal, him wanted to be different.
    changed.
saw a nigger conservative, him wanted to be different.
    changed.
niggers don't u know that niggers are different. change.
a doublechange. nigger wanted a double zero in front of
    his name; a license to kill,
niggers are licensed to be killed. change. a negro: some-
    thing pigs eat.
change. i say change into a realblack righteous aim. like
    i don't play
saxophone but that doesn't mean i don't dig 'trane.'
    change.
change.
hear u coming but yr/steps are too loud. change. even a
    lamp post changes nigger.
change, stop being an instant yes machine. change.
niggers don't change they just grow. that's a change;

bigger & better niggers.
change, into a necessary blackself.
change, like a gas meter gets higher.
change, like a blues song talking about a righteous to-
morrow.
change, like a tax bill getting higher.
change, like a good sister getting better.
change, like knowing wood will burn. change.
know the realenemy.
change,
change nigger: standing on the corner, thought him was
cool. him still
standing there. it's winter time, him cool.
change,
know the realenemy.
change: him wanted to be a TV star. him is. ten o'clock
news.
wanted, wanted. nigger stole some lemon & lime
popsicles,
thought them were diamonds.
change nigger change.
know the realenemy.
change: is u is or is u aint. change. now now change. for
the better change.
read a change. live a change. read a blackpoem.
change. be the realpeople.
change. blackpoems

will change:
know the realenemy. change. know the realenemy. change
        yr/enemy change know the real
change know the realenemy change, change, know the
        realenemy, the realenemy, the real
realenemy change your the enemies/ change your change
        your change your enemy change
your enemy. know the realenemy, the world's enemy.
        know them know them know them the
realenemy change your enemy change your change
        change change your enemy change change
change change your change change change.
your
mind nigger.

blackmusic/a beginning

pharaoh sanders
had
finished
playing
&
the whi-
te boy was to
go on next.

him didn't

him sd
that
his horn
was
broke.

they sat
there
dressed in
african garb
& dark sun glasses
listening to the brothers
play.   (taking notes)
we
didn't realize
who they
were un
til their
next recording
had been
released: the beach boys play soulmusic.

real sorry about
the supremes
being dead,
heard some whi

te girls
the other day—
all wigged-down
with a mean tan—
soundin just like them,
singin
rodgers & hart
& some country & western.

A Message All Blackpeople Can Dig
(& a few negroes too)

we are going to do it.
US: blackpeople, beautiful people; the sons and daugh-
        ters of beautiful people.
bring it back to
US: the unimpossibility.
now is
the time, the test
while there is something to save (other than our lives).

we'll move together
hands on weapons & families
blending into the sun,
into each/other.
we'll love,

we've always loved.
just be cool & help one/another.
go ahead.
walk a righteous direction
under the moon,
in the night
bring new meanings to
the north star,
the blackness,
to US.

discover new stars:
street-light stars that will explode into evil-eyes,
light-bulb stars visible only to the realpeople,
clean stars, african & asian stars,
black aesthetic stars that will damage the whi-temind;
killer stars that will move against
the unpeople.

came
brothers/fathers/sisters/mothers/sons/daughters
dance as one
walk slow & hip.
hip to what life is
and can be.
& remember we are not hippies,
WE WERE BORN HIP.

walk on, smile a little
yeah, that's it beautiful people
move on in, take over.   take over, take over take/over.
            takeovertakeovertakeover
        takeovertakeover   overtakeovertakeovertake over/
                take over take, over take,
        over   take, over   take.
blackpeople
are moving, moving to return
        this earth into the hands of

human beings.

We Walk the Way of the New World

        1.

we run the dangercourse.
the way of the stocking caps & murray's grease.
(if u is modern u used duke greaseless hair pomade)
jo jo was modern/ an international nigger
                born: jan. 1, 1863 in new york, mississippi.
his momma was mo militant than he was/is
jo jo bes no instant negro
his development took all of 106 years
& he was the first to be stamped "made in USA"
where he arrived bow-legged a curve ahead of the 20th

         century's new weapon: television.
which invented, "how to win and influence people"
& gave jo jo his how/ever look: however u want me.

we discovered that with the right brand of cigarettes
that one, with his best girl,
cd skip thru grassy fields in living color
& in slow-motion: Caution: niggers, cigarette smoking
                    will kill u & yr/health.
& that the breakfast of champions is: blackeyed peas & rice.
& that God is dead & Jesus is black and last seen on 63rd
            street in a gold & black dashiki, sitting in a pink
            hog speaking swahili with a pig-latin accent.
& that integration and coalition are synonymous,
& that the only thing that really mattered was:
         who could get the highest on the least or how to expand
         & break one's mind.

in the coming world
new prizes are
to be given
we *ran* the dangercourse.
now, it's a silent walk/ a careful eye
jo jo is there
to his mother he is unknown
(she accepted with a newlook: what wd u do if someone
         loved u?)

jo jo is back
& he will catch all the new jo jo's as they wander in & out
and with a fan-like whisper say: you ain't no
                                   tourist
                                   and Harlem ain't for
                                   sight-seeing, brother.

2.

Start with the itch and there will be no scratch. Study
     yourself.
Watch yr/every movement as u skip thru-out the southside of
     chicago.
be hip to yr/actions.

our dreams are realities
traveling the nature-way.
we meet them
at the apex of their utmost
meanings/means;
we walk in cleanliness
down state st/or Fifth Ave.
& wicked apartment buildings shake
as their windows announce our presence
as we jump into the interior
& cut the day's evil away.

We walk in cleanliness
the newness of it all
becomes us
our women listen to us
and learn.
We teach our children thru
our actions.

We'll become owners of the   New World
the New World.
will run it as unowners
for
we will live in it too
& will want to be remembered
as   realpeople.

Move Un-noticed To Be Noticed:
A Nationhood Poem

move, into our own, not theirs
into our.
they own it (for the moment) : the unclean world, the
                                    polluted space, the un-censor-
                                    ed air, yr/foot steps as they
                                    run wildly in the wrong
                                    direction.
move, into our own, not theirs
into our.
move, you can't buy own.
own is like yr/hair (if u let it live); a natural extension of
        ownself.
own is yr/reflection, yr/total-being; the way u walk, talk,
                        dress and relate to each other is *own*.
own is you,
cannot be bought or sold: can u buy yr/writing hand
                            yr/dancing feet, yr/speech,
                            yr/woman (if she's real),
                            yr/manhood?
own is ours.
all we have to do is   *take it,*
take it the way u take from one another,
        the way u take artur rubenstein over thelonious
            monk,

         the way u take eugene genovese over lerone bennett,
         the way u take robert bly over imamu baraka,
         the way u take picasso over charles white,
         the way u take marianne moore over gwendolyn
                  brooks,
         the way u take *inaction* over *action*.
move, move to act.   act.
act into thinking and think into action.
try to think. think.   try to think think think.
try to think. think (like i said, into yr/own) think.
try to think. don't hurt yourself, i know it's new.
try to act,
act into thinking and think into action.
can u do it, hunh? i say hunh, can u stop moving like a drunk
         gorilla?

                         ha ha   che che
                         ha ha   che che
                         ha ha   che che
                         ha ha   che che

move
what is u anyhow: a professional car watcher, a billboard for
         nothingness, a sane madman, a reincarnated clark gable?
either you is or you ain't!

the deadliving
are the worldmakers,
the image breakers,
the rule takers: blackman can you stop a hurricane?

"I remember back in 1954 or '55, in Chicago, when we had
13 days without a murder, that was before them colored
people started calling themselves *black*."
move.
move,
move to be moved,
move into yr/ownself, Clean.
Clean, u is the first black hippy i've ever met.
why u bes dressen so funny, anyhow, hunh?
i mean, is that u Clean?
why u bes dressen like an airplane, can u fly,
i mean,
will yr/blue jim-shoes fly u,
& what about yr/tailor made bell bottoms, Clean?
can they lift u above madness,
turn u into the right direction,
& that red & pink scarf around yr/neck what's that for Clean,
hunh?   will it help u fly, yeah, swing, swing   ing swing
            swinging high above telephone wires with dreams
            of this & that and illusions of trying to take bar-b-q
            ice cream away from lion minded niggers who
            didn't even know that *polish* is more that a
            sausage.
"clean as a tack,
rusty as a nail,
haven't had a bath
sence columbus sail."

when u goin be something real, Clean?
like yr/own, yeah, when u going be yr/ownself?

the deadliving
are the worldmakers,
the image breakers,
the rule takers: blackman can u stop a hurricane, mississippi
      couldn't.
blackman if u can't stop what mississippi couldn't, *be it. be it.*
blackman be the wind, be the win, the win, the win, win win:

      woooooooooowe boom boom   woooooooooowe bah
      woooooooooowe boom boom   woooooooooowe bah
if u can't stop a hurricane, be one.
      woooooooooowe boom boom   woooooooooowe bah
      woooooooooowe boom boom   woooooooooowe bah
be the baddddest hurricane that ever came, a black hurricane.
      woooooooooowe boom boom   woooooooooowe bah
      woooooooooowe boom boom   woooooooooowe bah
the badddest black hurricane that ever came, a black
           hurricane named Beulah,
go head Beulah, do the hurricane.
      woooooooooowe boom boom   woooooooooowe bah
      woooooooooowe boom boom   woooooooooowe bah
move
move to be moved from the un-moveable,
into our own, yr/self is own, yrself is own, own yourself.

go where you/we go, hear the unheard and do,
do the undone, do it, do it, do it *now*, Clean
and tomorrow your sons will
be alive to praise
you.

Re-taking the Takeable

to create or recreate an Afrikan mind
in a predominantly european setting   demands
serious work & has no wonder drug.
to recreate Afrikans is not a 12 week course
at UCLA with thanksgiving and christmas off
there will be no coffee breaks or 3 week vacations in the bahamas
we prepare to retake our minds   like
our enemies prepare for war.

we're trying to recapture
the substance & the future of ourselves
trying to recapture
the direction of our young.
it took a war to take them from us   and
it will take nothing less than a war
to return the minds of Afrikans
to their rightful owners.

LIFE-STUDIES

to hate one's self and one's people
is not normal
to perpetually wish to be like other people
is not normal
to act against one's self and one's community
is not normal
that
which is normal for us
will never be normal for us
as long as the abnormal   defines what
normality is.

WORLDVIEW:

fact is stranger than fiction
here in America in the year of 1973
many black people don't even know how
we came to this land

some black people believe that
we were the first people
to fly
and that we came first class.

Sources

Madhubuti, Haki R. (Don L. Lee). *Think Black!* Detroit: Broadside Press, 1966.

    "STEREO"
    RE-ACT FOR ACTION
    FIRST IMPRESSIONS ON A POET'S DEATH

Madhubuti, Haki R. (Don L. Lee). *Black Pride: Poems by Don L. Lee.* Detroit: Broadside Press, 1968.

    THE NEW INTEGRATIONIST

Madhubuti, Haki R. (Don L. Lee). *Black Words That Say: Don't Cry, Scream.* Detroit: Broadside Press, 1969.

    Gwendolyn Brooks
    But He Was Cool or: he even stopped for green lights
    DON'T CRY, SCREAM
    Malcolm Spoke/ who listened?
    a poem to complement other poems
    blackmusic/a beginning
    A Message All Blackpeople Can Dig

Madhubuti, Haki R. (Don L. Lee). *We Walk the Way of the New World*. Detroit: Broadside Press, 1970.

We Walk the Way of the New World
Move Un-noticed to be Noticed: A Nationhood Poem

Madhubuti, Haki R. (Don L. Lee). *From Plan to Planet | Life Studies: The Need for Afrikan Minds & Institutions*. Detroit: Broadside Press, 1973.

Re-taking the Takeable
LIFE-STUDIES
WORLDVIEW

dudley randall

Dudley Randall

Hilda Vest

Dudley Randall, founder of Broadside Press and Poet Laureate of Detroit, did not wear his heart on his sleeve. Instead, he was careful to tuck it away in his poetry as he moved through the many corridors of his life.

Born January 14, 1914, in Washington, D.C., Mr. Randall moved with his family to Detroit in 1921, where he created his poems in secret, since the icons of this bustling industrial city were more likely prizefighters rather than poets. Little did he know, at that young age, the power of the written word. Little did he know that he was destined to a permanent place at the center of the Black Arts movement of the 1960s.

Meeting Dudley Randall was by happy accident. While we were neighbors, living only a few blocks from each other, I had not realized the proximity until a friend asked him to read some of my poems after informing me that he lived "across the park" from her.

He invited me to participate in the Broadside Poets Theater, a monthly poetry reading which was held at Crummell Center in Highland Park. There were meetings in his home, which housed works of art, and, of course, lots of books. His wife, Vivian, was always cordial, and if I arrived early, she would show me a current acquisition of her lapidary collection. The meetings were designed to prepare for readings by such poets as Gwendolyn Brooks, Sterling Brown, Haki Madhubuti, Margaret Walker, Sonia Sanchez, and Etheridge Knight. I was awed by this distinguished circle of writers I had only known in books, and realized that a new world was opening up to me.

While Dudley was quiet, he was deliberate in his plans, and spoke as though his comments came only after considerable speculation. He announced, one day, after one of our meetings, that he had grown weary of the responsibilities required in running a publishing company, and had made plans to retire. That was the moment I decided to "reach for the torch." At the closing, he announced, to me and to my husband, Don, "Hilda, nobody buys poetry."

As the new owners, there were frequent phone calls to Dudley, who was now our consultant. "How much do we charge for permission to reprint a poem?" "Explain the policies of Baker & Taylor." "How do we get stores to accept our books on consignment?" "What about returns and credit?" His gratitude towards us for assuming the responsibilities of the Press was always evident as he quelled our concerns with patience and compassion.

He expressed his gratitude, also, by agreeing to make any public appearances I requested. He attended the program that concluded the Poet-in-Residence series where I had been facilitator for the Children's Library. He was attentive and relaxed as the children shared their poems that were printed in booklets they had just received. He accompanied Don and me to Chicago where Gwendolyn Brooks had invited us to receive the George Kent Award. When we arrived, Ms. Brooks was surprised to see Dudley, and announced that he had declined when she had invited him by phone. He participated in the twenty-fifth anniversary of Broadside Press, which was attended by Mayor Coleman Young. The mayor was in poor health by that time, and made few public appearances. He had hosted the tenth anniversary of the press, at which time, he gave the title of "Detroit's Poet Laureate" to Dudley Randall.

His sense of humor surfaced, at times, without warning. He had agreed to read at the Festival of the Arts. The poet before him danced during his performance. Dudley turned to me and whispered, " Am I going to have to dance?" Vivian often reminded me that she did not know how I did it, but I was able to garner a "yes" from him after he had told her that he was not going to participate in most of the events to which I had invited him.

He was also a mentor for my growth as a poet. Once I showed him a poem I had written in a style which was devoid of punctuation. He wrote in the margin, "Hilda, punctuation is not the scourge of some schoolmarm. It simply denotes the rise and fall of the human voice."

While he did not relish the limelight, once he was thrust into it, he soon forgot himself and enjoyed the interchange with beginning poets as well as with the seasoned ones.

Factory worker, US postal clerk, World War II veteran, husband, father, librarian, publisher, poet. All the time, observer! After the assassination of Malcolm X in 1965, the impact of the loss of this warrior led Randall to call for writers who wished to express what Malcolm's life had meant to them. He was overwhelmed by the response and was highly applauded as the editor (with Margaret G. Burroughs) of the anthology, *For Malcolm: Poems on the Life and the Death of Malcolm X* (1967), which includes the text of the eulogy by Ossie Davis.

1965 also marked the year of the first Broadside Press publication, "Ballad of Birmingham." This poem, originally published as a broadside, is perhaps Randall's most famous work. At least, it was the one most requested for permission to reprint during my tenure as publisher of Broadside Press. While gentle in many aspects, as was the poet, "Ballad of Birmingham" begins with no hint of the terror that lurks just outside the church, where safety dwells, or so we think. Suddenly, the imagery is stark as a mother hears an explosion.

"Ballad of Birmingham" was included in Dudley Randall and Margaret Danner's collaborative collection, *Poem Counterpoem* (1966), which consists of poems arranged in pairs in which the authors address similar themes such as love, old age, Africa, and oppression. In poems such as "Memorial Wreath," "Old Witherington," and "George," we see these larger social themes depicted through vivid imagery and the voices and lives of unique individuals.

Randall's keen powers of social observation are equally visible in his second collection of poetry, *Cities Burning* (1968), as he posits the plight of the Negro male and admonishes war in "Roses and Revolutions." Yet, we are left with a vision of what the world could and should be. In "Dressed All In Pink," we are seduced by color, believing in its innocence, only to be led to the tragic spot where "red," usually the symbol of life, is a stark symbol of death, President John F. Kennedy's blood stains on the suit of his wife, Jacqueline Kennedy.

Paul Breman, through his Heritage Series in London, featured Randall's *Love You* (1970). "The Profile on the Pillow," "The Brightness Moved Us Softly," and "My Second Birth" are examples of Randall's ability to profess love in a direct and passionate manner. Broadside Press distributed this series, which included such notables as Robert Hayden, Arna Bontemps, Conrad Kent Rivers, Mari Evans, and Russell Atkins.

More to Remember: Poems of Four Decades (1971), a publication by Third World Press, is dedicated to its publisher and Randall's prized pupil, Don L. Lee (Haki R. Madhubuti). This collection is divided into four sections: The Kindness and the Cruelty; Incredible Harvests; If Not Attic, Alexandrian; and Her Skin Deep Velvet Night. The poet chronicles his war experiences in "Pacific Epitaphs." He affirms "Black is beautiful" in "On Getting a Natural."

In *After the Killing* (1973), we observe the poet's constructive criticism of black militants in "Tell It Like It Is," and we watch slave become man in "Frederick Douglass and the Slave Breaker." "Green Apples" brings comic relief to the somber tones of "To the Mercy Killers," and it is to our advantage that they are included in the same collection. He concludes with a translation of "I Loved You Once," a poem by the Russian poet of African descent, Alexander Pushkin. I had not heard of Pushkin and often recall Dudley's chiding, "You call yourself a poet and you've never heard of Pushkin?" I hardly called myself "poet," but without a doubt, I quickly addressed my limited knowledge. This collection expresses Dudley Randall's variations of formal meter and free verse. Although not haiku, "For Gwendolyn Brooks, Teacher" is a prime example of concise word usage and is often read aloud by both scholar and neophyte.

In 1981, Naomi Long Madgett, publisher of Lotus Press, published *A Litany of Friends: New and Selected Poems*. This volume is divided into five sections and gives us a sense of Randall's varied life experiences. The first section, Friends, includes the title poem in which Randall expresses gratitude and thankfulness to the many friends who came to his rescue during a period of deep depression. "Poor Dumb Butch" teaches us about trust and "George" demonstrates courage and honor between two men of different generations. In Eros, Randall is baffled by the changing role of women in the sixties with his rendition of "Women" and "The New Woman." This collection includes "Bag Woman," a poem that forces us to think about how we are connected by our humanity regardless of our circumstances. One of the final poems in this collection is "A Poet Is Not a Jukebox," and is a concise retort to those who accused him of being less than militant.

Dudley Randall always had a keen sense of quality in the written word. One has only to look at the writers whom he nourished in the early years. His final contribution as publisher came in the form of *Homage to Hoyt Fuller* (1984), of which he was editor. From 1961 until 1976, Hoyt Fuller served as managing editor of John H. Johnson's *Negro Digest*.

In later years, it was known as *Black World*. Gwendolyn Brooks, Robert Hayden, Langston Hughes, LeRoi Jones, and John Williams were among the writers who made these publications worthy of the praise and acceptance they received. Included were book reviews and symposia on black literature. Fuller was in the process of compiling an anthology of selections from the earlier publications at the time of his death. Randall championed the cause and completed the work.

In 1999, Julius E. Thompson, director of the Black Studies Program at the University of Missouri-Columbia, published *Dudley Randall, Broadside Press, and the Black Arts Movement in Detroit, 1960-1995*. This account of Randall's contribution to literature includes photographs, tables, a bibliography, and detailed information on the evolution of the press. Thompson states in the preface: "His life's work serves as a model of the human possibilities still available in our own troubled times" (1).

Works Cited

Thompson, Julius E. Preface. *Dudley Randall, Broadside Press, and the Black Arts Movement in Detroit, 1960-1995*. By Thompson. Jefferson, North Carolina: McFarland & Company, Inc., 1999. 1-3.

Ballad of Birmingham

"Mother dear, may I go downtown
instead of out to play,
and march the streets of Birmingham
in a freedom march today?"

"No, baby, no, you may not go,
for the dogs are fierce and wild,
and clubs and hoses, guns and jails
aren't good for a little child."

"But, mother, I won't be alone.
Other children will go with me,
and march the streets of Birmingham
to make our country free."

"No, baby, no, you may not go,
for I fear those guns will fire.
But you may go to church instead,
and sing in the children's choir."

She has combed and brushed her nightdark hair,
and bathed rose petal sweet,
and drawn white gloves on her small brown hands,
and white shoes on her feet.

The mother smiled to know her child
was in the sacred place,
but that smile was the last smile
to come upon her face.

For when she heard the explosion,
her eyes grew wet and wild.
She raced through the streets of Birmingham
calling for her child.

She clawed through bits of glass and brick,
then lifted out a shoe.
"O, here's the shoe my baby wore,
but, baby, where are you?"

Memorial Wreath

(It is a little known fact that 200,000
Negroes fought for freedom in the Union
Army during the Civil War.)

In this green month when resurrected flowers,
Like laughing children ignorant of death,
Brighten the couch of those who wake no more,
Love and remembrance blossom in our hearts
For you who bore the extreme sharp pang for us,
And bought our freedom with your lives.

And now,
Honoring your memory, with love we bring
These fiery roses, white-hot cotton flowers
And violets bluer than cool northern skies
You dreamed of stooped in burning prison fields
When liberty was only a faint north star,
Not a bright flower planted by your hands
Reaching up hardy nourished with your blood.

Fit gravefellows you are for Douglass, Brown,
Turner and Truth and Tubman. . . . whose rapt eyes
Fashioned a new world in this wilderness.

American earth is richer for your bones;
Our hearts beat prouder for the blood we inherit.

Old Witherington

Old Witherington had drunk too much again.
The children changed their play and packed around him
To jeer his latest brawl. Their parents followed.

Prune-black, with bloodshot eyes and one white tooth,
He tottered in the night with legs spread wide
Waving a hatchet. "Come on, come on," he piped,
"And I'll baptize these bricks with bloody kindling.
I may be old and drunk, but not afraid
To die. I've died before. A million times
I've died and gone to hell. I live in hell.
If I die now I die, and put an end
To all this loneliness. Nobody cares
Enough to even fight me now, except
This crazy bastard here."

                And with these words
He cursed the little children, cursed his neighbors,
Cursed his father, mother, and his wife,
Himself, and God, and all the rest of the world,
All but his grinning adversary, who, crouched,
Danced tenderly around him with a jag-toothed bottle,
As if the world compressed to one old man
Who was the sun, and he sole faithful planet.

George

When I was a boy desiring the title of man
And toiling to earn it
In the inferno of the foundry knockout,
I watched and admired you working by my side,
As, goggled, with mask on your mouth and shoulders bright with sweat,
You mastered the monstrous, lumpish cylinder blocks,
And when they clotted the line and plunged to the floor
With force enough to tear your foot in two,
You calmly stepped aside.

One day when the line broke down and the blocks reared up
Groaning, grinding, and mounted like an ocean wave
And then rushed thundering down like an avalanche,
And we frantically dodged, then braced our heads together
To form an arch to lift and stack them,
You gave me your highest accolade:
You said: "You not afraid of sweat. You strong as a mule."

Now, here, in the hospital,
In a ward where old men wait to die,
You sit, and watch time go by.
You cannot read the books I bring, not even
Those that are only picture books,
As you sit among the senile wrecks,
The psychopaths, the incontinent.

One day when you fell from your chair and stared at the air
With the look of fright which sight of death inspires,
I lifted you like a cylinder block, and said,
"Don't be afraid
Of a little fall, for you'll be here
A long time yet, because you're strong as a mule."

A Different Image

The age
requires this task:
create
a different image;
re-animate
the mask.

Shatter the icons of slavery and fear.
Replace
the leer
of the minstrel's burnt-cork face
with a proud, serene
and classic bronze of Benin.

Dressed All in Pink

It was a wet and cloudy day
when the prince took his last ride.
The prince rode with the governor,
and his princess rode beside.

"And would you like to ride inside
for shelter from the rain?"
"No, I'll ride outside, where I can wave
and speak to my friends again."

They ride among the cheering crowds,
the young prince and his mate.
The governor says, "See how they smile
and cheer you where they wait."

The prince rides with the governor,
his princess rides beside,
dressed all in pink as delicate
as roses of a bride.

Pink as a rose the princess rides,
but bullets from a gun
turn that pink to as deep a red
as red, red blood can run,

for she bends to where the prince lies still
and cradles his shattered head,
and there that pink so delicate
is stained a deep, deep red.

The prince rides with the governor,
the princess rides beside,
and her dress of pink so delicate
a deep, deep red is dyed.

Roses and Revolutions

Musing on roses and revolutions,
I saw night close down on the earth like a great dark wing,
and the lighted cities were like tapers in the night,
and I heard the lamentations of a million hearts
regretting life and crying for the grave,
and I saw the Negro lying in the swamp with his face blown off,
and in northern cities with his manhood maligned and felt the writhing
of his viscera like that of the hare hunted down or the bear at bay,
and I saw men working and taking no joy in their work
and embracing the hard-eyed whore with joyless excitement
and lying with wives and virgins in impotence.

And as I groped in darkness
and felt the pain of millions,
gradually, like day driving night across the continent,
I saw dawn upon them like the sun a vision
of a time when all men walk proudly through the earth
and the bombs and missiles lie at the bottom of the ocean
like the bones of dinosaurs buried under the shale of eras,
and men strive with each other not for power or the accumulation of paper
but in joy create for others the house, the poem, the game of athletic beauty.

Then washed in the brightness of this vision,
I saw how in its radiance would grow and be nourished and suddenly
burst into terrible and splendid bloom
the blood-red flower of revolution.

The brightness moved us softly

Light flowed between black branches and new snow
into the shaded room and touched your eyes.
Your slow lids made another soft sun rise
upon your face, and as that morning glow
spread in your cheeks and blushed upon your lips,
the brightness moved us softly to a kiss.

My second birth

My second birth was when you came,
for all my years before
were only tranced awaiting of
your hand upon the door.

My christening was by your kiss,
and my real death shall be
upon that vast, world-ending day
when you have gone from me.

The profile on the pillow

After our fierce loving
in the brief time we found to be together,
you lay in the half light
exhausted, rich,
with your face turned sideways on the pillow,
and I traced the exquisite
line of your profile, dark against the white,
delicate and lovely as a child's.

Perhaps
you will cease to love me,
or we may be consumed in the holocaust,
but I keep, against the ice and the fire,
the memory of your profile on the pillow.

Anniversary Words

You who have shared my scanty bread with me
and borne my carelessness and forgetfulness
with only occasional lack of tenderness,
who have long patiently endured my faculty
for genial neglect of practicality,
for forgetting the morning and the parting caress
and for leaving rooms in a great disorderliness
which when I entered were as neat as they could be,

despite the absent-mindedness of my ways
and the not seldom acerbity of your tone,
I sometimes catch a softness in your gaze
which tells me after all I am your own
and that you love me in no little way.
But I know it best by the things you never say.

On Getting a Natural

(For Gwendolyn Brooks)

She didn't know she was beautiful,
though her smiles were dawn,
her voice was bells,
and her skin deep velvet Night.

She didn't know she was beautiful,
although her deeds,
kind, generous, unobtrusive,
gave hope to some,
and help to others,
and inspiration to us all. And
beauty is as beauty does,
they say.

Then one day there blossomed
a crown upon her head,
bushy, bouffant, real Afro-down,
Queen Nefertiti again.
And now her regal wooly crown
declares
I know
I'm black
AND
beautiful.

Pacific Epitaphs

RABAUL

In far-off Rabaul
I died for democracy.
Better I fell
In Mississippi.

NEW GEORGIA

I loved to talk of home.
Now I lie silent here.

TREASURY ISLANDS

I mastered the cards,
The dice obeyed me.
But I could not palm
The number on the bullet.

PALAWAN

Always the peacemaker,
I stepped between
One buddy armed with an automatic
And another with a submachine gun.

ESPIRITU SANTU

I hated guns,
Was a poor marksman,
But struck one target.

IWO JIMA

Like oil of Texas
My blood gushed here.

BISMARCK SEA

Under the tossing foam
This boy who loved to roam
Makes his eternal home.

TARAWA

Tell them this beach
Holds part of Brooklyn.

HALMAHERRA

Laughing I left the earth.
Flaming returned.

NEW GUINEA

A mosquito's tiny tongue
Told me a bedtime story.

LUZON

Splendid against the night
The searchlights, the tracers' arcs,
And the red flare of bombs
Filling the eye,
And the brain.

CORAL SEA

In fluid element
The airman lies.

BOUGAINVILLE

A spent bullet
Entered the abdominal cavity
At an angle of thirty-five degrees,
Penetrated the *pars pylorica*,
Was deflected by the *sternum*,
Pierced the *auricula dextra*,
And severed my medical career.

VELLA LA VELLA

The rope hugged tighter
Than the girl I raped.

LEYTE

By twenty bolos hacked and beat,
He was a tender cut of meat.

GUADALCANAL

Your letter.
These medals.
This grave.

BORNEO

Kilroy
Is
Here.

Poet

Patron of pawn shops,
Sloppily dressed,
Bearded, tieless, and shoeless,
Reading when you should be working,
Fingering a poem in your mind
When you should be figuring a profit,
Convert to outlandish religions,
Zen, Ba'hai and Atheism,
Consorter with Negroes and Jews
And other troublesome elements
Who are always disturbing the peace
About something or other,
Friend of revolutionaries
And foe of the established order,
When will you slough off
This preposterous posture
And behave like a normal
Solid responsible
White Anglo Saxon Protestant?

African Suite

1

SLAVE CASTLE
(Elmina, Ghana 1970)

Some were crying
    and some were cursing
Some were dry-eyed
    and some said never a
    mumbalin word

        when we stooped in the dark dungeons
        felt the chains and manacles
        stared at the cold grey waters
        tossing to frightful shores

Some were crying
some were cursing
some were dry-eyed
some said never a
mumbalin word

2

HOTEL CONTINENTAL
(Accra, Ghana)

Africa's
not considered
a continent
here.
While Europeans,
Americans,
Asians
dine,
the only Africans
in the room
are waiters.

3

HOTEL IVOIRE
(Abidjan, Ivory Coast)

Outside the hotel
a beautiful black girl
in a white bikini
lolls
in a billboard.

If she should step out of the billboard
to swim in the hotel pool,
she would gash her feet
on the broken glass
set in the concrete fence
the French erected
to keep the Africans
OUT.

4

VILLAGE GIRL
(Amasaman, Ghana)

Your black is deep
against the blue and white of your robe.
Your eyes are moons
in midnight Ghana sky.
The gems in your ears
are stars.

To The Mercy Killers

If ever mercy move you murder me,
I pray you, kindly killers, let me live.
Never conspire with death to set me free,
but let me know such life as pain can give.
Even though I be a clot, an aching clench,
a stub, a stump, a butt, a scab, a knob,
a screaming pain, a putrefying stench,
still let me live, so long as life shall throb.
Even though I turn such traitor to myself
as beg to die, do not accomplice me.
Even though I seem not human, a mute shelf
of glucose, bottled blood, machinery
to swell the lung and pump the heart—even so,
do not put out my life. Let me still glow.

Frederick Douglass and the Slave Breaker

I could have let him lash me
like a horse or a dog
to break my spirit.
Others never lifted a finger.
I would have been just one more.

But something in me said, "Fight.
If it's time to die, then die for *some*thing.
And take him with you."

So all day long we battled,
the man and the boy, sweating,
bruising, bleeding . . .

till at last the slave breaker said,
"Go home, boy. I done whupped you enough.
Reckon you done learned your lesson."

But I knew who it was that was whipped.
And the lesson I learned
I'll never forget.

Courage: A Revolutionary Poem

There are degrees of courage.
One person is not afraid to die.
A second is not afraid to kill.
A third is not afraid to be merciful.

For Gwendolyn Brooks, Teacher

You teach
without talk.

Your life
is lesson.

We give
because you do,

are kind
because you are.

Just live.
We will learn.

Green Apples

What can you do with a woman under thirty?
It's true she has a certain freshness, like a green apple,
but how raw, unformed, without the mellowness of maturity.

What can you talk about with a young woman?
That is, if she gives you a chance to talk,
as she talks and talks and talks about herself.

Her   self   is the most important object in the universe.
She lacks the experience of intimate, sensitive silences.

Why don't young women learn how to make love?
They attack with the subtlety of a bull,
and moan and sigh with the ardor of a puppy.
Panting, they pursue their own pleasure,
forgetting to please their partner, as an older woman does.

It's only just that young women get what they deserve.
A young man.

I Loved You Once
(Translated from the
Russian of Alexander Pushkin*)

I loved you once; love even yet, it may be,
within my soul has not quite died away.
But let that cause you no anxiety;
I would not give you pain in any way.
I loved you wordlessly, and hopelessly,
with jealousy, timidity brought low,
I loved you so intensely, tenderly
I pray to God some other love you so.

*Alexander Pushkin was the Russian poet of African descent who is credited for making the
Russian language live again.

Tell It Like It Is

Tell it like it is.
Lies won't get it.
Foaming at the mouth won't get it.
Defamation of character won't get it.

If you want to be virile,
be virile,
but you ain't gonna get virile
by saying somebody else ain't virile.
And if the white boys are all faggots,
like you say,
how come we got all these black poets
with yellow skin?

Blood Precious Blood

Blood
precious blood,
yours, Medgar,
yours, Malcolm,
yours, Martin,
flowing spreading sweeping
covering flooding drowning.

What can wash cleanse purify redeem this land
stained
with your blood,
your precious blood?

A Litany of Friends

For Vivian who snatched the shotgun out of my mouth,
Who walked by my side into the black pit and came out holding my hand,
Who shouted and scolded, cursed and wept, was patient and puzzled,
   silent and smiling until she led me out of the dark depths,

For Gwendolyn, my friend for ever, who remembered me and wrote
   me and sent gifts on Christmas and birthdays,
Who asked my friends to call me and write me and invited me to read
   and assured me that I was somebody,

For Don whose satire slashes but who was gentle and kind and opened
   his home to me,

For Safisha and Laini and Bomari, three beautiful loving people, who
   welcomed me with tenderness and trust,

For Hoyt who accepted and respected me as I was and not the hero I
   ought to be,

For Audre who wrote to me and sent donations from her readings,

For Sonia who called me and sent herbs and tea and scolded me for
smoking and laughed and joked when I was glum,

For June who sent me her book at a time when I needed reassurance,

For Etheridge who told me to live my pain and transcend it,

For Shirley who urged me to live and not to die,

For Lance who had faith in me and gave me his royalties and praised me,

For Naomi who assured me that my work was worthwhile,

For Robert who honored me with his friendship and confidence,

For Leonard who listened, and talked when I was silent,

For James and Marguerite who gave me the sanctuary of their home
where for a while I could forget,

For Jim who sent advice and for Jon who was kind and soft-spoken,

For Clyde who did not forget me and invited me to return,

For Melba whose faith in me gave me faith in myself,

For Arthur and Sarah who invited me to speak and argued and laughed
   with me,

For Todd who covered my class when I was afraid to appear before them,

For Joyce who wrote about me with empathy and invited me when I
   thought I was forgotten,

For Judy who called me and sobbed when I couldn't remember her name,

For Mildred who listened and talked to me when I was alone and afraid
   to go home to an empty house,

For Susie lover of dolphins who sent me a card and a note every Christmas,

For Carolyn who seldom wrote me, but who surprised me with an
   unexpected Christmas card,

For Walter, brother poet, who called me with concern and sent me a letter,

For Jean and Louise and Val who asked me to write a poem for them
   because they believed I would write again and for whom I wrote my
   first poem in five years,

For Malaika who invited me to live and work in Africa,

For Billy and Venita who asked to visit me and to spend the night with me,

For Phyllis and Ruby who called me when they needed help or advice,

For Evelyn who always kissed me when we met
(A touch, a hug, a kiss can save a life)

For Xavier who often called me and asked "What's going on?"

For Clifford who helped me recall my childhood,

For John who invited me to bowl and golf;

For all these ropes which pulled me to shore,

For these roots which anchored me against the wind and fed me from the
    past,

For the ties and integuments which bound me to them and them to me and
    fastened me to life,

For those who unfroze my tears and my laughter so that for the first time
    they flowed freely,

For all those who touched and hugged and kissed me
(A touch, a hug, a kiss can save a life),

For these, my thanks, my love,
And this litany of friends.

Poor Dumb Butch

Poor Dumb Butch,
Whom at first we called Wrinkle because of the white line that cavorted
    from your brow to your snout,
Who looked like a bear cub as a puppy and grew into a pony
Who knocked us down as you reared on your hind legs to welcome us,
Who scored 20 out of a possible 200 on your final exam in obedience
    training.

Poor Dumb Butch,
Yet you were better than I was.
You always outboxed me when I fought and wrestled with you,
Although your only fist was your slender nose,
And outran me when we chased each other around the yard,
And were always eager to walk with me through snow or rain,
And when in pain and incurably sick in your old age I took you to the
    veterinarian to kill you,
Your eyes glowed with love and anticipation as I fastened your leash.

The Ones I Love

The ones I love
Are not the beautiful,
The charming, the accomplished.
They have their meed
Of lovers.

If you are misunderstood, I will understand you.
If you are ugly, I will see your beauty.
If you are lonely, I will talk with you.

If you are hungry, I will feed you.
If you are naked, I will clothe you.
If you need, I will supply you.

You are the ones I love.

Loss

Your leaving is like a severed arm.
It   hurts. I reach to touch it.
Nothing's   there.

To Be In Love

To be in love: is to give
All, and never mind receive,
To learn your love and all her needs,
The slightest sign the lover heeds.
If she is sad, to make her smile,
And all her cares away beguile.

To be in love: is to enjoy,
As children with a treasured toy,
To trace the contours of her face
As maps of a beloved place,
Enjoy her body's lissome curves,
The bell-like music of her words,
The honey suckle of her breath,
And still adore her until death.

To be in love: is to be glad,
For love converts away from sad,
Rejoice at splendors of the world,
Sun, moon, and sky with stars impearled,
Enjoy birds' dawn and sunset cries,
And love each creature that's alive,
Because your love for her extends
To all the world and never ends,
Because your love for her extends
To all the world and never, never ends.

Women

I like women they're so warm & soft & sweet
Touch one & her skin yields like the flesh of a peach
Tall & short plump & slim old & young they come in fascinating shapes
Their breasts are round as oranges canteloupes melons
Soft smooth warm & kind to the cheek
Women smell so good fragrant as lilac or honeysuckle spicy as
    peppermint cinnamon sassafras
Their breath is fresh as the morning tangy as oranges mellow as black-
    purple grapes
Their walk is music their hips rhythm like bells
Their voices are an arpeggio of birds in April dawns or the low flute
    of a thrush
God made man first then woman correcting Her mistakes
And put her on earth to aspire and achieve and rejoice

The New Woman
(For M.H.W. and D.H.M., who said that my poem "Women" was sexist)

I like women they're so hard & tough & strong
Feel their muscle it's hard & hairy as a coconut
Doctors lawyers lumberjacks truck drivers wrestlers weight lifters
    bank robbers
There's nothing men do that women don't do better

Their fingers are quick as whips their lips rip out quips
Their brains are steel traps their mouths volley raps
They swear smoke pot & chew tobacco
Hawk & spit & collect art deco
They even open doors for themselves
Light their own cigars & sometimes men's
Wear pants not bras do they wear athletic supporters too
Seduce innocent men & rape them too
They do all the lousy things lousy males used to do

Only two things a man can be they cannot be
One is the dad of a large familee
Number two is with all their care
They cannot piss six feet straight up in the air

In all the rest they are the best

Yet while they govern nations take over corporations
Cut throats stab sisters in the back throw bosses on the rack
Engineer revolutions invent new solutions
This One Thing puzzles me & makes me groan

Where have all the women gone

In Africa

In Africa, in Africa
the strangers came and took the gold,
the emeralds and the diamonds,
the ivory and the slaves,
and paid for them in beads of glass
and cotton cloth and rum and gin.

In Africa in Africa
the strangers come & take the gold
& copper & petroleum
& bauxite & uranium
& pay for them with bicycles
& motor bikes & Citroens
& cinema & gin.

Bag Woman
(For Jane Hale Morgan)

Wearing an overcoat in August heat,
Shawls and scarves, a torn and dirty dress,
Newspaper shoes, she squats in the Greyhound terminal
And rummages through two bags, her lifetime treasure.

She mines waste baskets for her food and clothes,
Forages in the streets with sparrows, pigeons—
Isolate, with fewer friends than beggars have—
Another stray cat or abandoned dog,
She sleeps where cats and dogs sleep, in the streets.

Sister, once did you suck your mother's milk,
And laugh as she fondled you? Did Daddy
Call you his Dumpling, Baby Girl, his Princess?
And did you flirt with him, bending your head,
And, giggling, kiss his eyes through your long lashes?
Did some boy love you once, and hold you tight,
And hotly know you through a summer night?

Or were you gang-raped, violated early,
And from that trauma drifted down to this?
Or, born defective, abandoned to the streets?

Sister, I do not know. But I know that I am you.
I touch your rags, clasp your dumb eyes,
Talk with you, and drink your fetid breath.

A Poet Is Not a Jukebox

A poet is not a jukebox, so don't tell me what to write.
I read a dear friend a poem about love, and she said,
"You're in to that bag now, for whatever it's worth,
But why don't you write about the riot in Miami?"

I didn't write about Miami because I didn't know about Miami.
I've been so busy working for the Census, and listening to music all
    night, and making new poems
That I've broken my habit of watching TV and reading newspapers.
So it wasn't absence of Black Pride that caused me not to write about Miami,
But simple ignorance.

Telling a Black poet what he ought to write
Is like some Commissar of Culture in Russia telling a poet
He'd better write about the new steel furnaces in the Novobigorsk region,
Or the heroic feats of Soviet labor in digging the trans-Caucausus Canal,
Or the unprecedented achievement of workers in the sugar beet industry
    who exceeded their quota by 400 percent (it was later discovered to be a
    typist's error).

Maybe the Russian poet is watching his mother die of cancer,
Or is bleeding from an unhappy love affair,
Or is bursting with happiness and wants to sing of wine, roses, and
    nightingales.

I'll bet that in a hundred years the poems the Russian people will read,
     sing, and love
Will be the poems about his mother's death, his unfaithful mistress, or
     his wine, roses, and nightingales,
Not the poems about steel furnaces, the trans-Caucausus Canal, or the
     sugar beet industry.
A poet writes about what he feels, what agitates his heart and sets his
     pen in motion.
Not what some apparatchnik dictates, to promote his own career or
     theories.

Yeah, maybe I'll write about Miami, as I wrote about Birmingham,
But it'll be because I want to write about Miami, not because somebody
     says I ought to.

Yeah, I write about love. What's wrong with love?
If we had more loving, we'd have more Black babies to become Black
     brothers and sisters and build the Black family.

When people love, they bathe with sweet-smelling soap, splash their
     bodies with perfume or cologne,
Shave, and comb their hair, and put on gleaming silken garments,
Speak softly and kindly and study their beloved to anticipate and satisfy
     her every desire.
After loving they're relaxed and happy and friends with all the world.
What's wrong with love, beauty, joy, or peace?

If Josephine had given Napoleon more loving, he wouldn't have sown
   the meadows of Europe with skulls.
If Hitler had been happy in love, he wouldn't have baked people in ovens.
So don't tell me it's trivial and a cop-out to write about love and not about
   Miami.

A poet is not a jukebox.
A poet is not a jukebox.
I repeat, A poet is not a jukebox for someone to shove a quarter in his ear
   and get the tune they want to hear,
Or to pat on the head and call "a good little Revolutionary,"
Or to give a Kuumba Liberation Award.

A poet is not a *jukebox*.
A poet is *not* a jukebox.
A *poet* is not a jukebox.

So don't tell *me*   what to write.

When I Think of Russia

When I think of Russia, she will be
Not just two syllables to me,
But Anna Maslova and Igor,
Sonia, and Fikrat, and many more
With whom I've laughed and sung and talked,
Who gave to me their bread and salt,
The soft-eyed girl who took my hand
And led me through a red-scarfed band
While every smiling Pioneer
Cried, *"Mir i druzhba, druzhba i mir!"**
And I'll remember many another
Who clasped my hand and called me, "Brother! "

When I think of Russia, I shall see
A white ship on the Caspian Sea,
The wide straight streets of proud Moskva,
The flowers and hills of Alma Ata,
Leningrad's waters bright and blue,
And your million lights, Baku, Baku.
And neither time nor space shall part
These persons, places from my heart.

* "Peace and friendship, friendship and peace!"

Sources

Danner, Margaret and Dudley Randall. *Poem Counterpoem*. Detroit: Broadside Press, 1966.

Ballad of Birmingham
Memorial Wreath
Old Witherington
George

Randall, Dudley. *Cities Burning*. Detroit: Broadside Press, 1968.

A Different Image
Dressed All In Pink
Roses and Revolutions

Randall, Dudley. *Love You*. Heritage Series: Volume 10. London, Paul Breman: 1970.

The brightness moved us softly
My second birth
The profile on the pillow

Randall, Dudley. *More to Remember: Poems of Four Decades*. Chicago: Third World Press, 1971.

Anniversary Words
On Getting a Natural
Pacific Epitaphs
Poet

Randall, Dudley. *After the Killing*. Detroit: Broadside Press, 1973.

African Suite
To the Mercy Killers
Frederick Douglass and the Slave Breaker
Courage: A Revolutionary Poem
For Gwendolyn Brooks, Teacher
Green Apples
I Loved You Once
Tell It Like It Is
Blood Precious Blood

Randall, Dudley. *A Litany of Friends*. Detroit, Lotus Press: 1981.

A Litany of Friends
Poor Dumb Butch
The Ones I Love
Loss
To Be in Love
Women
The New Woman
In Africa
Bag Woman
A Poet Is Not a Jukebox
When I Think of Russia

sonia sanchez

Sonia Sanchez
Jessica Care Moore

Long silver locks wrapped behind a bandana replace her 1960s afro. She looks so many years younger than her age. Sonia Sanchez is alive and very much full of fire, words, and love for her people and her craft. She looks me directly in my eyes and asks if I have read *A Blues Book for Blue Black Magical Women* (1974). I remember that she has always been a champion for the feminine, fearlessly exploring women's lives, the triumphs of our history, and our conditions worldwide. She tells me she spent a year writing that Broadside Press book, reading the *Holy Quran, The Book of the Dead,* and *The Book of Masons* during the same time period. She explains that it is a difficult read and says that few reviewers really "got it."

She is holding court with a dozen young writers in my historical West End neighborhood in Atlanta. She speaks about James Baldwin, and how nervous she was when she met him for the first time: "I shook his hand and walked away." I tell her there are many of us who remember the first time she held our hands or offered us a word of advice. I'll never forget seeing Sonia and Amiri Baraka at a reading at the Schomburg Center in Harlem. They were joking and laughing together, as old friends do. A row of us younger poets sat in awe of these writers whom we had studied, surprised to find them so accessible. We love Sonia because she allows us to know her, to call on her.

Sonia's stories about her early speaking engagements in California, when young militant writers had to drive off with their headlights off until they hit the highway, intrigue me as I think of all the spoiled young poets who read their poems on television and wait to become "famous." Then there is the amazing circle of people she has pulled toward her light: Malcolm, Kwame Ture, Queen Mother Moore, Farrakhan. Her house was/is the house where everyone comes to eat, fight, talk, laugh, breathe. She provides the spiritual food and space for a community of writers, activists, people in search of a better world. And she's not done cooking yet—at least not poems. She is allowing others to take care of her a little more now. She has a chef who prepares her very strict vegetarian diet.

It is clear to me that she has offered her life to the Black Arts movement, to poetry, to freedom for oppressed people around the world. When she speaks of her friends and literary peers, she smiles and says they look at each other with surprise: "Like wow, you're still here?" Sonia Sanchez has been called many things—mother, warrior, sister, poet, activist, writer, playwright, lecturer, revolutionary. I would add survivor.

Born Wilsonia Driver on September 9, 1934 in Birmingham, Alabama, Sanchez grew up in Harlem, New York. She earned her BA in political science from Hunter College in 1955, and completed graduate courses at New York University (Academy of American Poets, par. 1). From the 1960s on, hers was a central voice in the African American liberation struggle. Her poems appeared regularly in *The Liberator*, *The Journal of Black Poetry*, *Black Dialogue*, and *Negro Digest*. They were fiery, impassioned, and political calls to action. They also were stylistically revolutionary. Sanchez's innovative use of Black English, musical rhythms, and unique line breaks and spacing characterized her poetry from the beginning. She and Haki Madhubuti (Don L. Lee) pioneered the effort within the Black Arts movement to make poetic language echo the sounds and rhythms of vernacular language within the Black community.

Her first book of poetry, *Home Coming* (Broadside Press, 1969), expresses outrage at white supremacist America. It exposes sexism, class conflicts, and the psychological effects of racism and slavery, offering a handbook for survival for African Americans. In the introduction, Haki Madhubuti comments: "Her ABC's were learned in alleys & corner bars; she knows what motivates her blk/sisters & she understands the hurt of the blackman. Her poems/poetry . . . is love poetry. The love of blackpeople, the love of blackness. That's what it's all about, the love of self and people. That's why/what Sonia writes" (7). Sanchez also confronts themes of inevitable death, pain, and loss in poems like "Malcolm":

> do not speak to me of martyrdom
> of men who die to be remembered
> on some parish day.
> i don't believe in dying
> though i too shall die
> and violets like castanets
> will echo me. (1-7)

In *We A BaddDDD People* (Broadside Press, 1970), Sanchez defiantly challenges Black people to refocus their attention away from white America and towards what they can do to free themselves. She points out the contradictions in the behavior of her brother activists in the Black Power movement. In "Blk/Rhetoric" Sanchez demands of all activists: "who's gonna make all / this beautiful blk/rhetoric / mean something":

> who's gonna give our young
> blk/people new heroes
>> (instead of catch/phrases)
>> (instead of cad/ill/acs)
>> (instead of pimps)
>> (instead of wite/whores)
>> (instead of drugs)
>> (instead of new dances)
>> (instead of chit/ter/lings)
>> (instead of a 35¢ bottle of ripple)
>> (instead of quick/fucks in the hall/way
>> of wite/america's mind)
> like. this. is an SOS
>> me. calling . . .
>>> calling . . .
>>>> some/one
>>> pleasereplysoon. (1-3, 26-42)

Sanchez also realized early on that the struggle for Black self-empowerment must include economic development. She understood how capitalism had affected the morality of African Americans, many of whom had been seduced by the materialism of American culture. In "Indianapolis/Summer/1969/Poem" she expresses frustration with the worship of money as god, a commentary that we find frequently in contemporary rap lyrics:

like.
    i mean.
        don't it all come down
to e/co/no/mics.
        like. it is fo
money that those young brothas on
illinois &
    ohio sts
        allow they selves to
be picked up
    cruised around
        till they
asses open in tune
        to holy rec/tum/
            dom.
& like. ain't it
    fo coins
        that those blond/
wigged/tight/pants/
        wearen/sistuhs
open they legs/mouths/asses
        fo wite dicks
to come
    in tune to (1-24)

The issues about which Sanchez wrote in her early poetry continue to be relevant to Black communities today and to inform her recent work. Yet, as with many great writers, Sanchez's poetic style has changed over the years. The tone of her more recent poems is less abrupt and demanding, and more reflective, exhortative, and celebratory. This is another lesson that I learned from Sonia. When I told her about people wanting me to return to a popular poem that I had written but felt I'd outgrown, she urged: "Keep writing. You're always getting better. Your audience has to grow with you."

Sanchez has published numerous volumes of poetry, plays, books for children, and has edited two poetry anthologies. She has lectured at hundreds of American universities and colleges and read her work all over the globe. In 1985 she was the winner of the American Book Award in Poetry for *Homegirls and Handgrenades* (1984). In 1997 her book *Does Your House Have Lions?* (1997) was a finalist for the National Book Critics Circle Award. She has been the recipient of many honors including a National Endowment for the Arts Award, a Pew Fellowship in the Arts, the Community Service Award from the National Black Caucus of State Legislators, and the Peace and Freedom Award from the Women's International League for Peace and Freedom. She held the Laura Carnell Chair at Temple University where she taught from 1977 until her retirement in 1999 (Academy of American Poets, par. 4-5). Most recently she has been awarded the Langston Hughes Award from City College of New York, the Robert Frost Medal by the Poetry Society of America, and the Harper Lee Award as Alabama's Distinguished Writer.

Anyone studying or reading Sonia Sanchez has to understand that she is not just an extraordinary poet. She is a warrior and natural healer for people around the world. Like Langston Hughes, she is a poet of the people, and for her people. Sanchez's work tells us to resist the oppressive ideas we have been taught, and create our own curriculum for living. Today she is one of the greatest examples of art as activism and activism as art. Poet Maya Angelou has deemed her "a lion in literature's forest."

I recently saw her power while at a conference in Johannesburg, South Africa, where she was on a panel with other African writers. They were discussing the importance of language and the teaching of indigenous languages in academic institutions. She listened patiently as the scholars debated whether Zulu or Swahili should be taught before French or English in South African schools.

When she finally spoke, the room changed. She described to the South African audience how Black students in the United States wage struggles with university administrators to demand that African Studies Departments be created and that African languages be taught. She also shared with the audience how, in the late sixties, the FBI had come to her home in San Francisco and harassed her for teaching the work of W. E. B. DuBois, Marcus Garvey, Langston Hughes, and Paul Robeson. These Black authors had not been taught at universities until scholars and educators like Sanchez incorporated them into their curricula. The FBI agents angrily accused her of being a "troublemaker"—she had dared to rescue the work of these "radicals" and "leftists" from what certainly must have been their planned obscurity. They even urged her landlord to throw her out of her home. The point she was making was how important it is for us to affirm our own heritage, whether it be the languages of South African peoples or the history and legacies of the African diaspora. She showed how our struggles are connected across time and continents.

I understood better after that day who Sonia Sanchez really is for African Americans. She represents the preservation and continuation of our culture. When future generations insist that institutions of higher learning recognize our scholars and writers, Sanchez's lifetime commitment to writing and organizing will have played a role.

As a young Black publisher and poet, I feel blessed to have had the opportunity to read my own work alongside this giant of American literature. I celebrate her undaunted spirit. A warrior understands it is never about the individual journey, but the legacy that continues to live on. Her words are alive in my head. Yes, Sonia! We continue to Resist. Resist. Resist. Resist. Resist. Reeeesisstt!

Works Cited

Madhubuti, Haki R. (Don L. Lee). Introduction. *Home Coming*. By Sonia Sanchez. Detroit: Broadside Press, 1969. 6-8.

"Sonia Sanchez." 14 Aug. 2001. The Academy of American Poets. 5 pars. 28 April 2004
        <http://www.poets.org/poets/poets.cfm?45442B7C000C040D0B>.

malcolm

do not speak to me of martydom
of men who die to be remembered
on some parish day.
i don't believe in dying
though i too shall die
and violets like castanets
will echo me.

yet this man
this dreamer,
thick-lipped with words
will never speak again
and in each winter
when the cold air cracks
with frost, i'll breathe
his breath and mourn
my gun-filled nights.
he was the sun that tagged
the western sky and
melted tiger-scholars
while they searched for stripes.
he said, "fuck you white
man. we have been
curled too long. nothing
is sacred now. not your

white faces nor any
land that separates
until some voices
squat with spasms."

do not speak to me of living.
life is obscene with crowds
of white on black.
death is my pulse.
what might have been
is not for him/or me
but what could have been
floods the womb until i drown.

to all sisters

hurt.
    u worried abt a
  little hurting.
        man
hurt ain't the bag u
    shd be in.
          loving is
the bag, man.
      there ain't
no MAN like a
     black man.
he puts it where it is
and makes u
     turn in/
       side out.

personal letter no. 2

i speak skimpily to
you about apartments i
no longer dwell in
and children who
chant their dis
obedience in choruses.
if i were young
i wd stretch you
with my wild words
while our nights
run soft with hands.
but i am what i
am. woman. alone
amid all this noise.

liberation/poem

blues ain't culture
                they sounds of
oppression
          against the white man's
shit/
   game he's run on us all
these blue/yrs.
             blues is struggle/
                        strangulation
of our people
            cuz we cdn't off the
white motha/fucka
             soc/king it to us
but. now.
        when i hear billie's soft
soul/ful/sighs
        of "am i blue"
               i say
no. sweet/billie
         no mo.
no mo blue/trains running on this track.
            they all been de/railed.
am i blue?
       sweet/baby/blue billie. no. i'm black/&
                        ready.

Blk/Rhetoric
(for Killebrew Keeby, Icewater, Baker, Gary Adams
and Omar Shabazz)

who's gonna make all
this beautiful blk/rhetoric
mean something.
                    like
i mean
        who's gonna take
the words
            blk/is/beautiful
and make more of it
than blk/capitalism.
                    u dig?
            i mean
                    like who's gonna
take all the young/long/haired
natural/brothers and sisters
and let them
            grow till
                    all that is
impt is them
            selves
                    moving in straight/
revolutionary/lines
            toward the enemy
(and we know who that is)

like. man.
who's gonna give our young
blk/people new heroes
     (instead of catch/phrases)
     (instead of cad/ill/acs)
     (instead of pimps)
     (instead of wite/whores)
     (instead of drugs)
     (instead of new dances)
     (instead of chit/ter/lings)
     (instead of a 35¢ bottle of ripple)
     (instead of quick/fucks in the hall/way
     of wite/america's mind)
like. this. is an SOS
    me. calling . . .
        calling . . .
           some/one
   pleasereplysoon.

Indianapolis/Summer/1969/Poem

Like.
     i mean.
          don't it all come down
to e/co/no/mics.
          like. it is fo
money that those young brothas on
illinois &
     ohio sts
          allow they selves to
be picked up
     cruised around
          till they
asses open in tune
          to holy rec/tum/
               dom.
& like. ain't it
     fo coins
          that those blond/
wigged/tight/pants/
          wearen/sistuhs
open they legs/mouths/asses
          fo wite dicks

to come
in tune to
there ain/t no
asses
like blk/asses
u dig?
and i mean.
like if brothas
programmed sistuhs fo love
instead of
fucken/hood
and i mean
if mothas programmed
sistuhs to
good feelings bout they blk/men
and i
mean if blk/fathas proved
they man/hood by
fighten the enemy
instead of fucken every available sistuh.
and i mean
if we programmed/
loved/each
other in com/mun/al ways
so that no
blk/person starved
or killed
each other on

a sat/ur/day nite corner.
then may
        be   it wud all
come down to some
                thing else
like RE VO LU TION
                i mean if.
                    like. yeh.

It's a New Day

we gon be
    outa sight black/men
    gon be part/
                panther
        gon be all Minister Farrakhan
                gon rap like RAP
    gonna teach like Elijah
      gon rule like Nyerere
            gon believe like King believed
            gonna be TCB/ing black men
as we walk in our red/yellow/suns

we gon be some
            beautiful/black/women
    gon move like the queens we be
    gon be full/
                time MUSLIM women

gon be strong as sojourner
gon be gentle as
                sister clotelle's smile
gon be the poetry of gwendolyn's words
gon be the green south of fannie lou hamer
gonna be warm as an african nite
while walken like songs

we gon be some badddDDD people
   just you wait and see
we gon be some badddDDD people
   just you wait and see . . . . . .

to P. J. (2 yrs old who sed write a poem for me in Portland, Oregon)

if i cud ever write a
poem as beautiful as u
little 2/yr/old/brotha,
i wud laugh, jump, leap
up and touch the stars
cuz u be the poem i try for
each time i pick up a pen and paper.
u. and Morani and Mungu
be our blue/blk/stars that

will shine on our lives and
makes us finally BE.
if i cud ever write a poem as beautiful
as u, little 2/yr/old/brotha,
poetry wud go out of bizness.

we can BE

we can be anything we want
for we are the young ones
walken without footprints
moven our bodies in tune
to songs
          echoen us. the beautiful
black ones.
         recently born.
               walken new
               rhythms
leaven behind us a tap dancer's dream
of sunday nite ed sullivan shows.
WE WILL BE
        ALL that we want
for we are the young ones
bringen the world to a Black Beginnen.

and it will be ours

we are a new people
look at us walk. we walken
A New Walk. Its beat is the sound of Elijah
hurryen us to new frontiers.
we be a new people in a new land.

we wear a new look
look at the style we wear. our clothes
demand your look. respect. for they tell
the land that a new people's garments
flow on the earth.
we be a new people in a new land.

our talk is new. it be
original talk always prefaced by
As-Salaam-alaikum (a greeting of peace)
for how else should we begin the day
save with peace for our people in a new land.
we be a new people in a new land.

we are a mixture of the old and new.
a new western man of ancient wisdom
openen the door of the world
while moven on a new land
in a new way.
we be a new people in a new land.

our leader is new. a man of the land
bringen us holy words for him all
praises are due Allah who came
bearen the truth of Islam for this
original man in this new land who
is multiplyen out loud.

and if we listen. ahhhh yes. and
if we listen. we new people
in this new land will be the rulers.
and it will be ours. and it will be ours.

PAST

1. woman

COME ride my birth, earth mother
tell me how i have become, became
this woman with razor blades between
her teeth.
              sing me my history O earth mother
about tongues multiplying memories
about breaths contained in straw.
pull me from the throat of mankind

where worms eat, O earth mother.
come to this Black woman. you.
rider of earth pilgrimages.
tell me how i have held five bodies
in one large cocktail of love
and still have the thirst of the beginning sip.
tell me. tellLLLLLL me. earth mother
for i want to rediscover me. the secret of me
the river of me. the morning ease of me.
i want my body to carry my words like aqueducts.
i want to make the world my diary
and speak rivers.

rise up earth mother
out of rope-strung-trees
dancing a windless dance
come phantom mother
dance me a breakfast of births
let your mouth spill me forth
so i creak with your mornings.
come old mother, light up my mind
with a story bright as the sun.

2. earth mother
(low singing is heard)

old/
woman's/
voice/

Bells. bells. bells.
let the bells ring.
BELLS. BELLS. BELLS
ring the bells to announce
this your earth mother.
for the day is turning
in my thighs And you are born
BLACK GIRL.

come, i am calling to you.
this old earth mother of the elaborate dreams
come. come nearer. girl. *NEARER.*
i can almost see your face now.
COME CLOSER.

Low/
laugh/

yes. there you are. i have stuffed
your whole history in my mouth
i. your earth mother
was that hungry once. for knowledge.
come closer. ah little Black girl
i see you.
i can see you coming
towards me little girl

running from seven to thirty-five
in one day.
i can see you coming
girl made of black braids
i can see you coming
in the arena of youth
girl shaking your butt to double dutch days
i can see you coming
girl racing dawns
i can see you coming
girl made of black rain
i can see you coming.

3. young/black/girl

Fivetenfifteentwenty
twentyfivethirtythirtyfiveforty
fortyfivefiftyfiftyfivesixty
sixtyfiveseventy
seventyfiveeighty
eightyfiveninety
ninetyfiveonehundredreadyornothere i come
REAdyornothereicome!
one
two
three. i see you.
        and you. and YOU. AND YOU.

AND YOU U U U U U U—step/mother.
woman of my father's youth
who stands at a mirror
elaborate with smells
all shiny like my new copper penny.
telling me through a parade of smiles
you are to be my new mother. and your painted lips
outlined against time become time
and i look on time and hear you
who threw me in angry afternoon closets
til i slipped beneath the cracks
like light. and time stopped.
and i turned into myself
a young girl breathing in crusts
and listened to those calling me.

to/   *no matter what they do*
be/   *they won't find me*
chanted/   *no matter what they say*
               i won't come out.

               i have hidden myself behind black braids
               and stutters and cannot be seen.

to/   *no matter what they do*
be/   *they won't find me*
chanted/   *no matter what they say*
               i won't come out

i listen to words asking
what did she say?
why can't she talk normal talk?
there's something wrong with that one!
she got the demon inside of her or something!
strange one!!
too quiet!!!

to/   *no matter what they do*
be/   *they won't find me*
chanted/   *no matter what they say*
                  i won't come out . . .

Coming out from alabama
to the island city of corner store jews
patting bigbuttedblack women in tune
to girlie can i help ya?
            girlie what you want today?
            a good sale on pork today.
            girlie.
                     girlie.
                            girlie.

coming out from alabama
to the island city of perpetual adolescence
where i drink my young breasts
and stay thirsty
always hungry for more than the

georgewashingtonhighschoolhuntercollegedays
of america.
>   remember parties
>   where we'd grindddddDDDD
>   and grindddddDDDDD
>   but not too close
>   cuz if you gave it up
>   everybody would know. and tell.
>   and grindddding was enough. the closeness
>   of bodies in project basement
>
>   recreation rooms was enough
>   to satisfy the platter's sounds
>   spinning you into body after body
>   then walking across the room
>   where young girls watched each other
>   like black vultures
>   pretending nothing had happened
>   leaving young brothers in conditions
>   they satisfied with out of the
>   neighborhood girls . . .

Coming out from alabama
into smells i could not smell
into nites that corner lights
lit dimly.

i walked into young
womanhood. Could not hear
my footsteps in the streets
could not hear the rhythm of
young Black womanhood.

4. young womanhood

And i entered into young
   womanhood. you asked.
   who goes there?

who calls out
   to this perennial
   Black man of ruin?

and time on her annual
   pilgrimage squatted and
   watched as i called
   out to love from my door.

what a lovely smell love
was. like a stream of
violets that warmed your face.

and i was found at the four
   corners of love. a Black
   man and I imprisoned
   with laughter at himself.

a man made sterile
by hatred
a famine man
starved and starving
those around him
in this plentiful country.

as i entered into my
young womanhood i became
   a budding of laughter. i
   moved in liquid dreams
   wrapped myself in a
   furious circuit of love
   gave out quick words
   and violent tremblings
   and kisses that bit
   and drew blood
   and the seasons fell
   like waterfalls on my thighs

and i dressed myself
in foreign words,
   became a proper painted
   european Black faced american
   going to theatre parties and bars
   and cocktail parties and bars
   and downtown village apartments
   and bars and ate good cheese
   and caviar with wine that
   made my stomach stretch for artificial warmth.

   danced with white friends who
   included me because that was
   the nice thing to do in the late
   fifties and early sixties

and i lost myself
down roads
i had never walked.

and my name was
without honor
and i became a
stranger at my birthright.

     *   *   *

who is that
making noise on this earth
while good people sleep
i wondered, as i turned
in our three year old bed of love.

in the morning
i reminded you of the noise
and you said,
just some niggers pretending

   to be the wind.

the nite brought more noise
   like a swift courier
   and i leaped from our bed
   and followed the sound.

   and visions came from the wall.
   bodies without heads, laughter without mouths.
   then faces crawling on the walls
   like giant spiders,
   came toward me
   and my legs buckled and
      i cried out.

one face touched mine and said:

   "you are a singer of songs
      but you do not listen to what men have said
      therefore you cannot sing."

a second face murmured:

   "you are a reader of books
      but books that do not teach you the truth
      are false messiahs."

a third face smiled as i closed my eyes:

   "you move as a free woman,
      but your body is a monument to slavery
      and is dead."

When morning came
you took me to
one inebriated with freud.

massaging his palms
he called out to me
a child of the south,
and i listened to
european words
that rushed out to
me and handcuffed
me.

And for awhile i rode
on horseback
among my youth
remembered southern days
and nites
remembered a beginning new york
girlhood where tall buildings looked
like aqueducts.
remembered stutters
i could not silence.

at the end of a month
when he couldn't explain
away continued acts that
killed.
at the end of a month
of stumbling alibis,
after my ancestral voices
called out to me against
past and future murders
i moved away from reconciling myself to
murderers
and gave myself up to
the temper of the times.

stood against discrimination
in housing.
jobs.
picketed. sat in. sang about
overcoming that which would
never come.
closed woolworths. marched
against T.V. stations while
ducking horseriding cops
advancing like funeral hawks.

was knocked to the ground
while my child screamed
at the cannibals on horseback.

and i screeeamed.
calling out to those who
would listen.

called out from carolinian
slave markets, mississippi
schools, harlem streets that
beasts populated us.
beasts with no human heartbeats
when they came among BLACKNESS.

and i vomited up the past.
the frivolous years and i
threw up the smiles and bowings
and nods that had made
me smile so many smiles.

and i vomited up the stench
of the good ship *Jesus*
sailing to the new world
with Black gold
i vomited up the cries of
newborn babies thrown
overboard

i vomited up the waters
that had separated me
from Dahomey and Arabia
and Timbuktoo and Muhammad
and Asia and Allah.

i vomited up denmarkvesey
and nat turner and rebellious
slave women
their big stomachs split open
in the sun.

i vomited up white robed choirs
and preachers hawking their sermons
to an unseeing God.

and i vomited out names like beasts.
and death. and pigs and death.
and devil and death
and the vomiting ceased.
and i was alone.

       *   *   *

woke up alone
to the middle sixties
full of the rising wind of history

alive in a country of echoes
convulsive with gods
alone with the
apocalypse of beasts,
in america. The repository
of european promise.
rabid america.
  where death is
  gay and obscene
  and legal in the sight
  of an unseeing God.

5. womanhood

Moving. constantly.
some destiny calling
out to me
   to explore the sea
   and the sky.
   to talk against
   sleeping on our knees.

and i moved.
eldest daughter of the womb.
eldest daughter of the world.

open to all Blackness
making the country keep in step
to these our new sounds.
to the music of a
million Black souls.

and i called out to prophesy
to make me a woman
of the beginning tribe
to make me a woman of
   tyrannical love to
   cover our wounds.

and
Blackness was the
order of the day.
all who looked were
enchanted and
chanted who they once were
and we fell down upon
the earth and became ourselves.

and
Blackness was the
order of the day
   and the voice of Elijah was
   heard opening the
   door of the world
   and all who came
   after him,
   poets and soothsayers
   rappers and raconteurs
   politicians and activists,
   writers and teachers,
   sang his wisdom.
   and we fell down
   upon the earth and
   became ourselves.

and
i gave birth to myself,
twice. in one hour .
i became like Maat,
unalterable in my
love of Black self and
righteousness.
and i heard the
trumpets of a new age
and i fell down
upon the earth
and became myself.

WE ARE MUSLIM WOMEN

WE ARE MUSLIM WOMEN
wearing the garments of the righteous
recipients of eternal wisdom
followers of a Divine man and Message
listen to us
as we move thru the eye of time
rustling with loveliness
listen to our wisdom
as we talk in the Temple of our Souls.

WE ARE MUSLIM WOMEN
triumphant before Allah
flooding the earth like emeralds
beautiful ones
becoming young in time
within Elijah's hands
giving birth to ourselves.
Sing praises to Him who
came in the person of Master Fard Muhammad.
Bow down upon the earth before Elijah
Lord of Almighty words,
for the earth hums as we walk
Allahuakbar—Allahuakbar—Allahuakbar   (to be sung)
and the Earth sings our gladness.

WE ARE MUSLIM WOMEN
dwellers in light
new women created from the limbs of Allah.
We are the shining ones
coming from dark ruins
created from the eye of Allah:
And we speak only what we know
And do not curse God
And we keep our minds open to light
And do not curse God
And we chant Alhamdullilah   (to be sung)
And do not curse God.

WE ARE MUSLIM WOMEN
dwelling in His hour
guardians of the gate of Islam
recorders of tomorrow
an adoration.

WE ARE MUSLIM WOMEN
moving in the ark of time
women of a million years
passing thru the Door of the World
Sing praises to Him who
came in the person of Master Fard Muhammad
bow down upon the earth before Elijah
the Lord of our changing Seasons
for the earth hums as we walk
Allahuakbar—Allahuakbar—Allahuakbar
And the earth sings our gladness

Sources

Sanchez, Sonia. *Home Coming.* Detroit: Broadside Press, 1969.

> malcolm
> short poem
> to all sisters
> personal letter no. 2

Sanchez, Sonia. *Liberation Poem.* Broadside No. 34. Broadside Series. Detroit: Broadside Press, 1970.

> liberation/poem

Sanchez, Sonia. *We A BaddDDD People.* Detroit: Broadside Press, 1970.

> Blk/Rhetoric
> Indianapolis/Summer/1969/Poem

Sanchez, Sonia. *It's a New Day: (poems for young brothas and sistuhs)*.
Detroit: Broadside Press, 1971.

It's a New Day
To P. J. (2 yrs old who sed write a poem for me in Portland, Oregon)
we can BE
and it will be ours

Sanchez, Sonia. *A Blues Book for Blue Black Magical Women*. Detroit:
Broadside Press, 1974.

woman
earth mother
young/black/girl
young womanhood
womanhood
We are Muslim Women

Epilogue: The Dudley Randall Center for Print Culture

> The age
> requires this task:
> create
> a different image;
> re-animate
> the mask. . . .
>
> (Dudley Randall, "A Different Image" 1-6)

In May of 2001 a tribute ceremony honoring Dudley Randall was held at the University of Detroit Mercy. Mr. Randall worked at the University of Detroit as a reference librarian and served as our esteemed poet-in-residence in the late sixties and seventies. From 1969 until shortly before his death, he judged the annual student poetry contest which bears his name. At the ceremony, UDM's McNichols campus library was designated a national literary landmark by the Friends of the Library, USA in recognition of Dudley Randall's extraordinary contributions to the fields of US literature and publishing.

A second dedication, that of The Dudley Randall Center for Print Culture (DRCPC)—a new electronic publishing classroom and production lab—also took place that day.[1] Our naming of the Center after Dudley Randall stemmed from our deep appreciation of the contributions Mr. Randall had made to UDM students and the University as a whole over the years, as well as our great respect for his achievements. It also reflected our commitment to joining the many other individuals who are carrying forth his vision of the written word as a vital art form intimately connected to self-determination, and of publishing as a vehicle for building communities and promoting cultural critique.

In attendance at the ceremony were many of these writers, publishers, scholars, community activists, and members of the Randall family: Mrs. Vivian Randall, Phyllis Randall Sherron, Mr. Randall's daughter, and other relatives; Detroit Poet

Laureate and Publisher of Lotus Press, Dr. Naomi Long Madgett; Donald and Hilda Vest, former editors and owners of Broadside Press; Betty Boone, Executive Director of the Michigan Council for Arts and Cultural Affairs; Dr. Melba Boyd, poet, producer and director of the documentary *The Black Unicorn: Dudley Randall and the Broadside Press* (1996), and author of the biography, *Wresting with the Muse: Dudley Randall and the Broadside Press* (2004); poet and professor Dr. Gloria House as well as poet and community leader, Albert M. Ward, both of whom were named the Center's first Writers-in-Residence at the ceremony. Also in the audience that day were the student winners of the 2000-1 Dudley Randall Poetry contest, and numerous other writers, artists, and friends who had worked with or been touched in some way by this great man.

The inclusive spirit of that day continues to infuse the mission of the DRCPC: to eliminate the boundaries traditionally drawn in the field of publishing between student, community, and academic writers; between creative and scholarly work; and between print and electronic media. This is a new model of university pedagogy and publishing, one made possible by new technologies that enable individuals to create the types of publications that once took entire companies to produce. It is a model based on the belief that the *process* of creating, circulating, and consuming texts is as valuable as the end product itself. The Dudley Randall Center for Print Culture is committed to introducing young writers, editors, and publishers to the artistic and social power of the written word, and to providing them with the training to make use of that power; we are committed to serving as a resource center for writers throughout our metro area; we are committed to exploring and using new publishing technologies and venues to produce innovative scholarly research and creative works.

Thus, on any given day you may find students in the Center taking classes in writing for print and the Web or in editorial processes and products. They may be designing the latest issue of UDM's student arts journal, or collaborating with their professors on our chapbook series of student and community creative writing. Faculty members may be editing articles and multi-media projects for *Post Identity*, an online academic journal of the humanities. Center Writers-in-Residence, authors, and UDM Press staff are likely to be meeting to discuss the latest project proposal or to plan an event for the Center's Writers on Writing series, which hosts free lectures, roundtables, and workshops for campus and Metro Detroit area writers. English professors, students in our Creative Writing track, and secondary education faculty may be organizing a creative writing workshop for local area high school students. Many tasks are being undertaken; many different images created.

In this time of shrinking state and university budgets it is important to note that these activities and publications are made possible only through the joint efforts of members of Detroit area creative writing communities and institutions; University administrators, faculty, and students; and local philanthropic organizations. Authors, editors, publishers, and professors volunteer their time and expertise to lead events and workshops. UDM provides course releases, stipends, and course credits for faculty and students working on Center publications. Almost all of our publications are funded through grants from outside institutions.

This anthology and accompanying CD, a joint publication of Broadside and UDM Presses, were made possible by grants from the McGregor Fund, the Michigan Council for Arts and Cultural Affairs (a partner agency of the National Endowment for the Arts), the Impact Foundation, and by the volunteer editorial work provided by the Broadside Board of Directors and UDM faculty. The CD was recorded and engineered by Masterpiece Sound Studios, which is owned by former Motown writer and producer, Sylvia Moy, and manufactured by Millennium Disc. Strongly committed to education and the arts, both Masterpiece and Millennium provided these services at rates significantly lower than the industry standard. Permissions to publish and record the poets' work were generously granted by the poets themselves—Haki Madhubuti and Sonia Sanchez, or by their heirs and executors—Nora Brooks Blakely, the Dudley Randall Estate, Janice Knight Mooney, and the Charlotte Sheedy Literary Agency. JEB (Joan E. Biren), Lynda Koolish, Robert Turney, Willie Williams, the University of Michigan Special Collections Library, and the Spelman College Archives provided us with the photographs that accompany the poets' work. The UDM Library and Special Collections staffs assisted our research greatly. Each author we approached to write the introductory essays enthusiastically accepted our request. Literally dozens of other individuals also contributed their time, energy, and expertise to making A Different Image a reality.

Certainly the support of these individuals and institutions stemmed from their appreciation of the literary and cultural legacy of Broadside Press—a legacy which is founded on a community-based model of publishing. For those of us who strive to provide new, experimental, or non-mainstream writers with a means of reaching audiences who appreciate their work, the forty-year history of Broadside Press is a powerful source of inspiration: to start with the printing of a single poem on an 8 ½ x 11 sheet of paper and to develop a list of over one hundred titles that includes some of the most important authors and works of the twentieth century, to publish aesthetically and culturally revolutionary work, to accomplish this largely through the efforts of one man who was joined by many other writers, readers, and activists who contributed their passion and labor to the fulfillment of these goals—this is the legacy of Broadside Press.

We want *A Different Image* to serve as a source of inspiration for the writers, readers, students, scholars, and publishers who read it. We invite you to join us and the other individuals committed to carrying forth this extraordinary legacy.

Rosemary Weatherston, Ph.D.
Director, Dudley Randall Center for Print Culture

Endnotes

[1] The Center was established in October 2000 under the leadership and vision of Professor Hugh Culik and with a generous grant from the McGregor Fund, a foundation that supports programs in education and human services in southeastern Michigan.

Acknowledgements

We wish to thank the following organizations and individuals for their contributions to and support of the Broadside Legacy project:

For generous funding support:
The McGregor Fund
The Michigan Council for Arts and Cultural Affairs, a partner agency of the National Endowment of the Arts
The Impact Foundation

For gracious permission to reprint poems:
Nora Books Blakely
The Dudley Randall Estate
Janice Knight Mooney
© The Estate of Audre Lorde, reprinted by permission of the Charlotte Sheedy Literary Agency
Haki R. Madhubuti
Sonia Sanchez

For gracious permission to reprint photographs:
The Special Collections Library, University of Michigan, Ann Arbor, for the photographs of Gwendolyn Brooks and Dudley Randall
Robert Turney, for the photograph of Etheridge Knight
JEB (Joan E. Biren) and the Spelman College Archives, for the photograph of Audre Lorde
Lynda Koolish, for the photograph of Haki Madhubuti
Willie Wiliams, for the photograph of Sonia Sanchez
(All photographs © 2004)

For brilliant production of the companion CD:
Carlos Gunn of Masterpiece Sound Studios

For the beautiful design of the anthology:
Dr. Timothy Dugdale

For the loan of the mask used for cover art:
Mr. and Mrs. Albert M. Ward

For their ongoing support:
Vivian Randall and Phyllis Randall Sherron
Hilda and Donald Vest
Dr. Richard Donelan, Sondai K. Lester, Lindiwe
Lester, Dr. Aombaye Ramsey, Tene Ramsey, and
Willie Williams, Members of the Broadside Board of
Directors
Dr. Naomi Long Madgett
Dr. Melba Boyd
Jessica Care Moore
Hugh Culik
Betty Boone and Carol Culham, Michigan Council for
Arts and Cultural Affairs
Sylvia Moy, Anita Moy, and Dr. Barbara Wilson of
Masterpiece Sounds Studios
Michael Grace of Millennium Disc
Kathleen Dow and Franki Hand of the Special
Collections Library, University of Michigan, Ann
Arbor
Taronda Spencer of the Spelman College Archives
The staff of the Special Collections Archive,
University of Detroit Mercy

Father John M. Staudenmaier, Acting Dean of UDM's
College of Liberal Arts and Education
Adrian Kerrigan and Barbara Bammarito, UDM
Department of Advancement
Jane Hoener, Director, Wayne State University Press
Cheryl Corey, McNaughton Gunn, Inc.

Gloria House, Ph.D,
Rosemary Weatherston, Ph.D.
Albert M. Ward

a different image recitations

albert m. ward • gloria house

Gwendolyn Brooks
01 kitchenette building
02 when you have forgotten Sunday: the love story
03 love note I: surely
04 Malcolm X
05 To Don at Salaam
06 Paul Robeson
07 A Black Wedding Song
08 Horses Graze

Etheridge Knight
09 He Sees Through Stone
10 The Idea of Ancestry
11 To Make a Poem in Prison
12 Belly Song
13 This Poem
14 For Black Poets Who Think of Suicide

Audre Lorde
15 For Each of You
16 Equinox
17 Black Mother Woman
18 The Seventh Sense
19 Conclusion
20 Revolution Is One Form of Social Change

Haki Madhubuti
21 Gwendolyn Brooks
22 But He Was Cool or: he even stopped for green lights
23 DON'T CRY, SCREAM
24 blackmusic/a beginning
25 We Walk the Way of the New World
26 Re-taking the Takeable

Dudley Randall
27 George
28 A Different Image
29 Roses and Revolutions
30 The profile on the pillow
31 For Gwendolyn Brooks, Teacher
32 The Ones I Love.
33 Bag Woman

Sonia Sanchez
34 malcolm
35 personal letter no. 2
36 liberation/poem
37 Blk/Rhetoric
38 It's a New Day
39 to P. J. (2 yrs old who sed write a poem for me in Portland, Oregon)
40 we can BE